CONTENTS

Listening to Children

Talking with Children about Difficult Issues

Nancy Close
Yale Child Study Center

Allyn and Bacon

Boston • London • Toronto • Sydney • Tokyo • Singapore

To my husband, Gene, who is my inspiration. To my own children, Jonathan and Matthew, who have clearly taken me along as a very proud participant as they have led the way in their development and to all of the children who have given me the privilege of listening to them.

Managing Editor: *Steve Dragin*
Series Editor: *Traci Mueller*
Series Editorial Assistant: *Bridget Keane*
Marketing Manager: *Amy Cronin*
Production Editor: *Annette Pagliaro*
Composition Buyer: *Linda Cox*
Manufacturing Buyer: *Suzanne Lareau*
Cover Administrator: *Kristina Mose-Libon*
Electronic Composition: *Publishers' Design and Production Services, Inc.*

Copyright © 2002 by Allyn & Bacon
A Pearson Education Company
75 Arlington Street
Boston, MA 02116
Internet: www.ablongman.com

Library of Congress Cataloging-in-Publication Data

Close, Nancy, 1950–
    Listening to children : talking with children about difficult issues /
Nancy Close.
      p. cm.
    Includes bibliographical references.
    ISBN 0-205-32648-X
    1. Interpersonal communication in children. 2. Communication in the family. 3. Parent and child. 4. Children and adults. I. Title.

BF723.C57 C58 2002
155.4′136—dc21   2001046381

Printed in the United States of America

10 9 8 7 6 5 4 3 2 1   05 04 03 02 01

PREFACE

Many years ago, when I was a young kindergarten teacher, I had a supervisor who always seemed to be able to encourage children to talk with her about anything, including difficult issues such as strong negative feelings or the death of a grandparent. After hearing such conversations, I would go to my journal as soon as possible and try to write down exactly what she said to encourage the children to talk. I soon learned (with her help) that the magic did not come from her words but, rather, from what the children were telling her and how she used their words to help them ask questions or share their feelings. My supervisor was a sensitive and thoughtful observer of children's behavior, and she had a way of using these observations when she engaged in conversation with children. I then turned my focus away from trying to parrot my supervisor's words and toward becoming a careful observer of young children. Since those days of being a young teacher, I have become a parent, a child therapist, a university professor, and a consultant. In all of these roles, I have focused on using observation to shape the way in which I communicate with children. I observe how children behave, and I listen to what they say before I begin to talk.

It is my hope that this book will reach a wide audience, including college students, teachers of young children, family and child therapists, pediatricians, nurses, and parents. My goal in writing this book is simple. I want the people who encounter young children to be able to encourage them to communicate and talk about everyday issues as well as sensitive and difficult issues. I want adults to feel comfortable talking about death, fears, pregnancy, and birth with young children, and I want adults to have faith in what children may know or think about these issues so they can hear what they are saying or asking. It is this kind of faith that is easily communicated to children and that can really start them talking. Once children feel comfortable talking and asking about any topic, they feel understood and the possibilities for communication are endless. We do know that children who feel understood and are able to communicate their thoughts and feelings in adaptive ways are likely to continue to be thinking, feeling, and interactive individuals.

Before we turn specifically to what children are telling us about various topics, we need to explore information concerning the cognitive, social, emotional, and language development of young children. The remaining chapters in the book explore issues that seem to be most significant for this age group. Chapter 3, "I Am Afraid the Dark Will Keep Me Night Night," explores common fears expressed by preschoolers. Chapter 4, "I Feel Like Killing My Mommy," discusses dealing with angry, aggressive, and rageful feelings. Chapter 5, "When You Die, Can I Live in Your House?" explores children's understanding of death, separation, and loss. Chapter 6, "I Think the Law is Right about Whales," explores how to help children to express and extend their conceptual knowledge about the world. Chapter 7, "I Am Going to Hate That Baby for the Rest of My Life," brings us to that much-discussed topic of siblings. Chapter 8, "This Is Very Important. When I Am Four and I Am a Man, I Will Get a Car," explores the wishes and disappointments of preschoolers as well as issues of self-esteem.

In all of the chapters, I delineate the basic points concerning each issue and why these particular issues are so important to children. I also discuss ways of helping children to express themselves on these issues. I use examples of children's conversations, questions, and thoughts throughout all of the chapters. Although some of the responses to and interpretations of children's questions and comments are directly connected to theoretical and empirical data, many of them come from my own experiences of working clinically and educationally with children over a 30-year period. My particular style of responding to children may or may not resonate with the students, teachers, or parents who read this book. All of us need to develop our own voice, focus, and style when speaking with young children. What needs to remain constant across all styles is the need to allow children to know that their thoughts and questions are meaningful and that when they express their thoughts or questions, someone is listening and interested in what they have to say—no matter how difficult the topic may be.

The insights and the expertise of the following reviewers were extremely helpful in the process of writing this book: Barbara Gillogly, American River College; Nancy Hughes, University of Central Florida, and Robert Pasnak, George Mason University.

1 Listening to Children

Introduction

I recently attended a baby shower for a friend where experienced mothers were asked to offer advice to the new parents. One of the bits of wisdom my husband and I offered was to say, "Have faith in the force of development. Let your child lead the way while you offer love, support, confidence, and guidance." One of the ways children can lead the way is through what they say to us. The main objective of this book is to convince the readers; parents, teachers, and all those adults who interact with young children to have faith in and respect for what children have to tell us and to respond to them appropriately and respectfully. There are ways to help children to tell us about issues that are important to them. For young children aged 2 to 5, these issues include common fears, dealing with anger and aggression, siblings, birth and death, growing up and its accompanying wishes and disappointments, and learning about the world.

Before exploring how children between the ages of 2 and 5 can talk to us about issues that are important to them, it is necessary to describe some characteristics common to this age group and some of the typical issues that cause them difficulty. Children in this age group are struggling to be independent and autonomous but are still quite unconvinced that they are. They may at one moment obstinately insist on being completely in control while at the next moment be completely fearful, helpless, and demanding. Normally developing children of this age have invested in relationships with important people (i.e., parents or primary caregivers) and have a sense of trust in themselves and others. They also care about how these important others respond to them and their behaviors and thoughts. Despite this, children in this age group are very egocentric, both in their thinking and behavior, and it is not unusual to hear a 4-year-old say, "Maya can't have any because I want to play with them now." As children become more verbal, they are able to think symbolically, but this thinking has a very rigid quality. "You have to get off the swing because I'm stronger than you." Preschoolers also begin to realize that there are reasons to explain most events and the existence of people and things in their world. However, their reasons have a very egocentric flavor. For example, "The sun is shining because it wants to."

Jonathan, Age 3

Why, then, is it important to encourage children to talk and engage in conversation with us? Is it so we can make them more rational and less egocentric? That may be a long-term goal, but remember that we should have faith in the force of development; if we do, we know that children eventually become more rational, altruistic, and flexible both in their thinking and in their relationships. Therefore, we encourage them to talk for a number of other reasons. When children talk, they can be helped to mediate action (i.e., express an angry thought in words rather than in a hit, kick, or bite). Children also talk to solve conflicts, ask questions, seek reassurance, and express thoughts and feelings. Adults may often think, "Oh, preschool children don't think about topics such as birth, death, the reasons for things." But when we really listen to children, we learn that they have lots of thoughts and information. They may have accurate information, inaccurate information, and/or distorted information. Thus, when children talk and ask questions, we are given the opportunity to clarify

Emily, Age 4

information for them. If we express interest in what they are saying rather than saying something such as, "Oh, the sun can't think about shining," then children gradually develop the confidence in their ability to express themselves and, as a result, have the opportunity to gain new information and, most important, feel understood.

Conclusion

Throughout this book I will emphasize three important components of talking with young children. We must always be respectful and interested in what they have to say. We have to speak to them at their level, and we must be careful not to overwhelm them and ask them too much or give them more information than they can handle.

A recent study sponsored by the National Research Council and the Institute of Medicine (Shonkoff & Phillips, 2000) focuses on important information about the first 5 years of life. The main finding is that children are constantly aware of and reactive to their environment. They can be depressed and are seriously affected by the mood of their caregivers or the quality of their environment. It has been found that positive influences during the first 5 years of life can have a long-lasting and positive influence on a child's development. In light of this study, it is interesting to examine the results of a concurrent study by DGY, Inc. (2000), which found that parents are misinformed about raising young children. Some of this misinformation is shocking. Sixty percent of the parents of young children think that 6-month-old babies can be spoiled if adults pick them up when they cry. Babies must have their cries and needs responded to in order to develop basic trust in themselves and their world (Erikson, 1950). Sixty percent of parents condone spanking as a regular form of punishment; however, research indicates that spanking leads to aggression and bullying. These are just two bits of the knowledge gap that indicate how crucial it is to be knowledgeable about development in the early years in order to be able to listen to children and understand what they are saying.

CHAPTER

2 Overview of the Development of Young Children

Developmental Overview

Young children have rich and complicated inner lives. They have wishes, dreams, confusions, conflicts, worries, and strong feelings. Their ability to be in touch with their inner lives depends on their development in the areas of social, emotional, cognitive, and language development. Adults who interact with children need to be informed about how children develop in each of these areas. When they are informed, adults are able to understand and respond when children ask questions that may seem difficult to answer. Adults who understand how children think, feel, and communicate are able to find ways of answering children's questions so that children extend what they ask and develop in all areas. The developmental topics of attachment,

5

separation, affective expression and regulation, cognition, language, and play are explored in this chapter.

Attachment and Separation

Attachment Theories.   There are many theoretical views of how attachments develop. Some believe that a newborn's sensitivities to the scent of mother's milk and the sound of her voice may promote attachment. Some babies are thought of as being temperamentally predisposed to forming attachments. Cognitive theorists think children must develop some form of object permanence before being capable of developing attachments. Behaviorists see that when a primary caregiver meets an infant's needs, the caregiver becomes an important conditioned reinforcer. Harlow (1959), in his studies of monkeys separated from their mother, found that the monkeys sought some kind of contact comfort either from one another or from a cloth monkey. Thus, he concluded that there probably is a more basic motive for attachment. Ethologists (Bowlby, 1969; Robertson, 1953) believe that attachment is a fixed-action pattern, which is triggered by a releasing stimulus during a critical period. Critical periods in development recently received wide attention in the media. The results of brain research indicated that a caring, protective, and stimulating environment in the first few years of life can support the most optimal brain growth whereas an adverse environment or the experience of abuse or neglect can lead to a slowing of brain development. Thus, it is clear that attachments are formed as a result of a variety of factors. Infants appear to be biologically programmed to attach. The environment that responds to their basic biological needs must be loving, sensitive, and consistent so that they can develop a sense of basic trust, cognitively develop concepts of object permanence, and begin to become separate and independent.

Early Attachments.   Infants develop from being sleepy, reflexive, and helpless newborns into walking, talking, feeling, thinking, and semi-independent children by the time they are 5 years old. There is a tremendous amount of development in the first 3 months of life. Observe a 3-month-old lying on his or her back interacting with an adult who is handing over a rattle. If you only watch for 5 minutes, you may see the baby smile and coo at the adult, roll over, and grab the rattle. In this observation, you will see the rapid development occurring in the areas of developing relationships, coordinating actions and motor control, vocalizing, and expressing affect. Although the baby is quickly developing in all areas, the baby is especially developing his or her relationship with the adult caregiver. If you watch the baby's response to a familiar adult, you will see the wide smiles and arms and legs moving with wild excitement. You can almost feel the intensity of the attachment to an important caregiver. Once this is seen, it is then easy to understand the central role human relationships have in development (Provence, 1977). Infants are born preferring to look at human faces and listen to human voices. Research has shown that a newborn recognizes his or her mother's voice and the smell of her breast milk. In other words, newborns come into the world ready to attach and relate to others. It is also generally agreed that an infant's early experience with a caregiver has an enduring significance for the development of interpersonal relationships (Freud, 1965; Ainsworth, 1978). It is this first relationship that enables children to develop mutually satisfying relationships with others. If it is a predictable, consistent, and loving relationship, then infants develop a sense of basic trust in themselves and others (Erikson, 1950). It is this sense of basic trust that then allows toddlers to work toward developing a sense of separateness and independence (Mahler, 1975) and autonomy (Erikson, 1950).

Growth toward Independence. When young children have enough investment in relationships with others and have developed a sense of basic trust and a positive sense of themselves, they are motivated to develop control over their impulses; this leads to the development of inner controls (Freud, 1965). As toddlers and young preschoolers are working on becoming more independent from their parents, they are constantly working on dealing with an intense mixture of love and aggression. In a predictable, caring, and developmentally supportive environment, they eventually learn to be less self-centered and are able to maintain loving feelings and loyalty even when they are disappointed in or angry with their loved ones. They normally learn that their anger can be expressed and will not harm anyone (Greenacre, 1960). Once preschoolers have developed more self-control, they can better tolerate frustration; they become more considerate in their relationships with others, thus preparing themselves to enter the world of peer relationships. They also begin to internalize the attitudes and values of their parents. This allows children to keep a connection to their parents as they are becoming more independent and self-sufficient.

Quality of Attachment. Attachment is usually measured by a child's efforts to maintain contact or proximity to a caregiver, a child's expression of anxiety about being separated from a primary attachment figure, and a child's reaction to a reunion with his or her parent(s). Ainsworth, Blehar, Walters, and Well (1978) developed an empirical paradigm that has been used to measure the quality of a child's attachment. They found that children can be classified as securely or insecurely attached. In the latter category, there are three subcategories; avoidant, resistant, and mixed avoidant resistant. Securely attached children are found to interact affectionately with others and are less likely to cry when separated from their parents. As older children, they are happy, socially competent, and active and self-reliant in school. Ainsworth and others found that children's patterns of attachment can change as family conditions change and interpersonal relationships change.

Process of Attachment. The process of attachment begins at birth. Up until 3 months of age, an infant's attachment behavior appears fairly indiscriminate. By 3 to 4 months, infants begin to select familiar people over strangers, and by 6 to 7 months a baby's attachment is clearly established and evidenced by an intensified dependence on the primary caregiver. This is often the period of time when happy, smiling babies begin to cry when mother or father leaves the room or when an out-of-town grandparent arrives expecting to see wide smiles. By 15 months, most infants move into toddlerhood. They are usually active and extremely excited over their newfound ability to walk. The child's love for the primary caregiver usually spreads to include his or her entire world and his or her own activities. Hence, the young toddler is often described as "being in love with the world." Once toddlers develop representational intelligence and the ability to walk, they begin to realize the need to separate from their primary caregivers. This is both an exciting and painful process, called the rapprochement phase, which is usually completed by age $3\frac{1}{2}$ (Mahler, 1975).

Separation. It is clear that in positive attachment relationships children need to gradually become separated and individuated from their parents. Dealing with separation is a lifelong process in which the final separation is death. Those who study attachment and separation (Ainsworth et al., 1978; Bowlby, 1969; Mahler, 1975; Robertson, 1953) acknowledge that a normal reaction to experiences of loss and separation is some mixture of protest and anger about separation as well as anxiety about other separations. Children do have real, strong, and painful experiences over being separated from their parents. This can occur when a 3-year-old goes to nursery school for the first time; a toddler gets a new babysitter; an adolescent goes off to college; a busy and preoccupied parent goes into another room without telling her preschooler where she is; and even when a veteran day-care child is feeling particularly vulnerable. Because we all have an inborn instinct to protect our children from danger, we may wonder why we subject our children to such experiences. Is there anything we can do to protect them from having such harsh feelings? We do a disservice to both our children and ourselves to even think we can avoid having children experience these inevitable feelings. They are, indeed, very natural, and when children are helped to acknowledge, accept, understand, express, and cope with these feelings, their affective lives are enriched and they can move on developmentally. In addition, when children are helped to master these anxieties about separation, they are more able to address anxieties or questions about death.

Development and Reactions to Separation.   Separation experiences and the accompanying feelings have different meanings for children, depending on their developmental level. At each developmental level, children have different skills available to them to help them cope with separation. When we teach college students studying psychology about separation, we ask them to think about their most recent major separation experience, leaving home to go to college. As young adults leaving home, they have a history of separation experiences that they have dealt with in either adaptive or nonadaptive ways. They have many memories of their parents, families, homes, and friends. They often understand when they have ambivalent feelings and are able to express them. They have the ability to conjure up a fairly detailed mental portrait of their loved ones, and they have some idea of the growth that occurs with the development of independence.

Influences on Coping with Separation.   Although adolescents have many skills to aid in coping with the pain of separation, at times they still need to work very hard to cope. Younger children also have to work hard to cope with separations, and their skills are not as developed as the teenagers'. In general, there are several factors that influence the way a child copes with experiences of separation and loss. The most common experience younger children have is the daily separation they must make from their parents when they attend day care. Factors that affect a child's ability to cope with feelings of separation anxiety include the quality of a child's relationship with his or her primary caregivers; the child's developmental level; previous separation experiences; the quality of a day-care program; and connections between home and family that are made for the child when he or she is away from home. The goal for all those who help children to cope with separation anxiety is to help them to keep an inner tie to the primary caregiver. The amount of help a child needs with this task varies according to his or her developmental level and emotional well-being. For example, a preschool child may have more difficulty coping with separating from mom and going to school just after mom has returned from the hospital with a new baby. Sometimes children surprise us and show no difficulty coping with the aforementioned scenario, but have a delayed reaction a few weeks later, after adjusting to the idea of having a younger sibling and feeling comfortable enough to experience and express ambivalence toward both the baby and the parents.

Separation Reactions of Preschool Children.　Preschoolers have many capacities that support them in coping effectively with separations (Provence et al., 1977). Many of them have had successful separation experiences such as going to day care, staying with a babysitter while their parents go away, etc. They have fairly well-developed language skills so that they can be encouraged to talk and ask questions about the separation, such as, "Where will you be? When will you come back? Who will take care of me? I don't like it when you go to work." We may find it painful to hear these questions or comments, but language is a skill children can use to cope with separation anxiety. Preschoolers also have the capacity to think and play symbolically (Erikson, 1950; Freud, 1965; Piaget, 1952). This allows them to maintain a mental portrait of their parents and, also, through imaginative play, become the person they are missing. In these ways, children are able to maintain a connection to home. Preschoolers have a fairly good capacity for object constancy, that is, they understand that if something is hidden from their sight it still continues to exist (Piaget, 1952). This conceptual ability applies to the constancy of both things (Piaget, 1952) and people (Freud, 1965; Mahler, 1975). Thus, preschoolers are able to be away from their parents and think about where they are and what they are doing. Engaging in this kind of thinking can clearly help a young child cope with feelings of separation anxiety.

Separation Reactions of Toddlers. Toddlers are just beginning to use language, think symbolically, and establish their sense of object constancy and permanence. They need more help than preschool children do to keep an inner tie to their parents when they are separated. Toddlers benefit from having concrete reminders from home (i.e., pictures of their homes and families, a special blanket or teddy bear, etc.). They are also helped when adults talk to them about their anxieties about separation (i.e., "I know you do not like it when I go to work. You wish I could stay with you. I will pick you up at the end of the day. I know you will have a good time with your teachers and friends today. I will think about you when I am at work today. I miss you too when I go to work."). These kinds of comments acknowledge that toddlers may have strong feelings about separation. They give them a model for putting their own feelings into words. Toddlers love games of hiding and finding things as well as filling up containers and dumping them out. These kinds of games help them to be in control of the appearance and disappearance of things when they do not have control of whether their parents come or go. They also help toddlers work on the development of object constancy and permanence. Thus, although these games look tedious and boring to adults, they are a means by which children master anxieties about separation and develop cognitive skills.

Separation Reactions of Infants. Very young infants have not yet differentiated themselves enough from their caregivers to experience anxiety over separation. They do, however, experience a change in the caregiving environment when they begin day care or when their primary caregiver leaves for all or part of each day. Infants do not have the language, cognitive skills, and play skills that toddlers and preschoolers have, but they do have an innate interest to attach and relate to others. Thus, it is clear that although infants may not experience separation anxiety, they do need consistent, predictable, and loving caregiving to promote the development of attachments and trust in themselves and important caregivers. They need to be cared for in an environment where their needs are met and their frustration level does not go above what they are developmentally able to cope with.

The Influence of Other Developmental Stages on the Process of Attachment. The idea that development in all areas occurs in phases or stages is useful in understanding how growth in the various domains of development is a complex process in which the various areas of development are complexly interrelated and continually affect one another. Stages progress from undifferentiated states to more complex states. To truly understand development, it is important to be knowledgeable about all of the phases and stages and how they relate to one another. Several theorists describe phases and stages for various areas of development. Piaget (1952) described the stages of cognitive development beginning in infancy with sensorimotor thinking, proceeding through preoperational thought in the preschool years, concrete thought in the school-age years, and through adolescence with the development of abstract thinking. Erikson (1950) described eight stages of psychosocial development from infancy through adulthood. The important stages in the first 5 years foster the development of basic trust, autonomy, and initiative. Margaret Mahler (1975) described the stages of the separation/individuation process during the first 3 years of life from the autistic phase, symbiotic phase, practicing phase, and rapprochment phase, through the phase in which children develop a sense of separateness and independence as well as a positive sense of self.

In the area of the development of attachment and separation, consider the 7-to-9-month-old infant who, according to Mahler, is just emerging from a symbiotic state with his primary caregiver and realizing his separateness from this caregiver. Piaget, who described the cognitive stages of development, said that at the age of 7 months, a baby is not yet completely able to understand that when objects disappear, they continue to exist. If that object becomes emotionally charged (e.g., a caregiver), it is easy to understand the stranger anxiety babies experience at this age. If one examines Erik Erikson's psychosocial theory of development, which describes the child's development within a social framework, one can see that a baby of this age is struggling with the issue of trust vs. mistrust. Thus, the child's management of this stranger anxiety depends on how well the environment has been capable of protecting the child from being overwhelmed by inner and outer stimuli.

Children's Separation Responses. When we watch, listen to, and talk to young children, how do we know they are thinking about issues connected to separation and attachment? Obviously, the children who are not yet verbal will communicate with us through various behaviors. These behaviors may include crying, clinging to a parent, becoming angry, or looking sad and withdrawn when they anticipate or experience a separation from a primary caregiver. Similar kinds of behaviors may occur when the children are reunited with their parents. It is important for adults to realize that even if these behaviors persist and are difficult, they are not a result of a child being spoiled or manipulative. The behaviors are the ways children express their anxiety about separation. Adults then need to put some of these feelings into words for children. They need to say things such as, "I know you don't like it when I go away from you, but you really will be all right. You may be feeling sad and mad at me for going." These kinds of comments give children a framework for understanding their inner responses and feelings connected to becoming more separate and independent. Older preschoolers, between 3½ and 5 years of age, are usually able to articulate their feelings about separation and independence, but still need adults to listen to the comments they may make. Even when children are just beginning to use language, they may use simple phrases that indicate something about their work in the area of attachment and separation. Consider the young 2-year-old who refers to her mother and herself as "me mommy mom." Clearly those three words illustrate the task of separation individuation that this child is

Will, Age 5, "Castle"

working so hard to accomplish. She wants to be just "me," but she also wants to be "me mommy." She wants to be independent, but she is not yet ready to completely give up her special and dependent relationship with her mother. Now consider the 3-year-old who is looking to more emulate and identify with his father while he is trying to separate from his mother. He calls himself "Daddy's big boy" and "Mommy's baby." He will not allow himself to be called "Daddy's baby" or "Mommy's big boy." Here, one sees how rigid the thinking of young children can be. It also is clear that this little boy wants to become more separate and independent and is appropriately looking to emulate his father to ease the process. At the same time, he realizes he still needs the reassurance of being Mommy's baby to be able to accomplish this. He does not need to be told, "Oh, you are not a baby; you are a big boy." Rather he needs to be told, "It is sometimes hard work being a big boy. You know even big boys sometimes have baby feelings." This kind of statement allows him to be able to talk about the struggle between independence and dependence he is facing and perhaps express the mixture of anger, excitement, and sadness that children facing this task of development experience.

Affective Development

The ways in which young children express feelings related to the demands of separation and independence as well as other developmental demands depends on a number of factors. First, there are two major ways in which the developmental literature conceptualizes the ability to express affect. Some (Bridges, 1932; Sroufe, 1979) proposed that there is profuse excitement at birth which differentiates according to the child's cognitive development and social interactions. Others (Izard, 1991) proposed that several discrete emotions are present at birth, even if they are not all expressed at once. Campos and colleagues (1988) described newborns as being capable of expressing joy, interest, disgust, and distress. Stenberg, Campos, and Emde (1983) and Izard and Malatesta (1987) showed that by the time babies are 8 months old, the affects of surprise, anger, fear, and sadness are added to the affective repertoire. By 18 months, children experience embarrassment, empathy, pride, shame, and guilt.

Secondly, at birth there are individual differences in temperament expressed by motility patterns and state regulation. Bornstein (1999) contended that temperament is a child's style of behaving and responding emotionally to people and events. Chess and Thomas (1977) described the three types of temperaments as being easy, difficult, and slow to warm up. More recent studies (Rothbart & Bates, 1998) characterized temperamental styles as positive affect and approach, negative affectivity, and effortful control. Others (Goldsmith & Gottesman, 1981) found that environment interacts with temperament and, thus, experience can lead to a change in style. In general, however, temperamental styles seem to be stable over time and do affect the way children express affect (Chess & Thomas, 1977).

Third, by the age of 18 months, children are able to express several discrete emotions. Children begin to actually label feelings between 20–24 months and label feelings in themselves and others by 28 months (Bretherton & Beeghly, 1982). Children do express their feelings in different ways. Some are easy to read and others are more difficult. Some children's expression of affect is well modulated whereas others express feelings in intense or muted ways. All of these ways of expressing affect are within the normal range (Provence, Naylor, & Patterson, 1977). In general, the child's ability to express and control affect depends on the stability of his or her relationship with significant caregivers. The more stable, consistent, and secure the relationship is, the more children will be able to tolerate and express all levels of feelings. Children do need to feel that their feelings are understood and that adults are willing to help them figure out how they are feeling if they are overwhelmed or confused by a particular feeling. Children often look to their caregivers' faces to determine what their emotional response should be (Walden, 1991). Feinman and Lewis (1983) even found that babies watch their mother's emotional reaction to a stranger before they respond.

Discussing Feelings with Children

Children need adults to label their feelings for them. Although children, 3–5 years of age are able to match labels of feelings to pictures of various affects, they do have difficulty with actually naming the feelings (Michalson & Lewis, 1985). Therefore, they often understand feelings more than they can talk about them. Adults need to be careful when they label children's feelings. They need to know a child's particular way of expressing affect. Sometimes what looks like anger can be anxiety and what looks like sadness can be anger. Also, children need to be included in the process of figuring out how they might feel at any given time and whether the feeling is a response to an internal or an external event. It is never useful to say to a young child, "Well, why did you do that?" or "How does that make you feel?" Children do not always know how they feel. They feel especially confused when they are experiencing a mix of feelings. Harter and Whitesell (1989) found that young children cope with one feeling at a time and become "confused with a mix of emotion." The typical mixes they feel are anger and sadness, love and hate, excitement and anxiety, and confidence and vulnerability. They sometimes experience these feelings in very intense ways, and they often do not know what to do with the intensity of feeling. We often see young children become more active or engage in difficult behavior when they are overwhelmed by strong and opposing feelings.

It is hard to help some young children modulate intense feelings before they have adequate words to mediate their tendency to act out. Even with children who are only putting two words together, it is important for adults to use language to help them understand their feelings. Saying something such as, "You have some very big and strong angry feelings today," after a child has had a tantrum may be helpful in helping him begin to make connections between his feelings and behavior. This may not stop tantrums or angry outbursts, but it will give the child a guide for beginning to understand, express, and cope with a variety of feelings.

The process of helping children to express their feelings does not begin when they are verbal. It begins early in infancy, as primary caregivers work to understand what a baby's various cries mean. These cries become identified as the tired, hungry, wet, anxious, or bored cries. A parent may say to an infant who is angry about having had to wait for a bottle and who is sucking the bottle while his sobs gradually subside, "You were really angry you had to wait so long for your bottle. You were so hungry and maybe worried mommy would not come to get you." Although the baby may not understand all of the words, he may understand his mother's attempt to soothe him and help him to make some sense out of his experience. Just as parents soothe a distressed baby, they also can comment on a baby's glee, happiness, or excitement. Saying things such as, "Oh, what a big smile. You like it when daddy talks to you," also gives a baby an affective message. Babies listen and respond to the comments their parents make. They hear the affect in the parents' voices and either become comforted or excited. Parents and infants often create an affective dance together (Brazelton, 1983), in which they take turns opening and closing the channels of affective communication. It is this kind of reciprocity that lays the foundation for older children to be able to trust and understand a particular affect and to be able to express it in ways that are eventually understood by themselves and others.

As mentioned before, children react to situations, people, or feelings in their own individual ways. When they are experiencing and expressing feelings, children are also constrained by their particular phase of development. A child's stage of cognitive development does affect the way he or she understands and reacts to his or her own and others' feelings. Consider the following scene during a discussion among children in kindergarten. John came to the meeting feeling very angry with some of the children in the class because they would not agree to use only his ideas while they were building with blocks. John announced at meeting, "I have a list, and on that list I am going to write down the names of everyone who was mean to me. I am going to put my list under my Christmas tree. When Santa sees it, he will not bring any of those kids Christmas presents." Geordie, who was most unwilling to let John dominate the play, looked panic-stricken as he turned to his teacher and said, "I hope John does not know how to spell my name." Geordie, like other 5-year-olds, assumed that because John said something, it would happen, and, thus, was genuinely worried that Santa would not bring him presents. Geordie was clearly in the preoperational phase (Piaget) of cognitive development. His thinking was egocentric, based on perception, and more magical than realistic.

Cognitive Development

Infancy

Jean Piaget, a pioneer in the field of the cognitive development of children, developed a theory that views children as actively constructing knowledge through their constant exploration and manipulation of their world. His theory describes the ways in which children mentally represent their world and manipulate a symbol system at various ages and stages. His theory is based on detailed observations of his own children. He described the growth of cognitive development as proceeding from simple reflexive activity in infancy to complex abstract and logical thinking in adolescence.

Piaget's descriptions of cognitive development in infancy focus on the ways in which inborn reflexes, such as sucking, grasping, visual tracking, and turning toward a sound become more goal directed and refined over the first year of life. Initially, an infant's cognitive responses are purely sensiormotor and have little coordination or intention. Observe a 2-to-3-month-old who is lying on his or her back, watching a rattle suspended in the air by a parent. The baby usually looks at the rattle and will visually follow it from side to side. She may reach out her hands and try to grab the rattle, but may swipe at it. She may kick her legs and wave her arms more to try to get it, but she may not be able to grab it unless the adult puts it right in her hand. Now look at this child at 4 to 5 months. She can probably grab that rattle, bring it to her mouth, explore it, and maybe even shift it from hand to hand. This rapid development is due to both an inner drive to manipulate and master the world (White, 1960) and the availability of a responsive, consistent, trustworthy, and stimulating world. It is this kind of interaction between the child and his or her environment that, according to Piaget, allows a child to construct the knowledge of his or her world. When older infants demonstrate reactions to the world that are no longer purely reflexive, it is clear that their behavior is goal oriented and involves an awareness of past events.

Toddlerhood

As children reach the age of 18 to 24 months, they begin to show the ability to use mental representation in many ways. They begin to engage in simple symbolic play, usually of domestic mimicry such as pretending to feed a baby doll and put it to bed. They show that they can use simple trial and error to solve simple problems. Observe a 2-year-old completing a three-piece form puzzle. After she has completed it, an adult can turn it so that the forms are not lined up with the holes. Most likely, the child can see this and will adapt the fitting of the forms to the changed position of the board. Children of this age also engage in something that Piaget called deferred imitation. The example often cited is that of children who imitate a tantrum they may have witnessed another child having in day care. This kind of behavior indicates that children of this age have the capacity to store mental images.

Preschool Children

Children move out of the sensiormotor stage into the preoperational stage of cognitive development (Piaget, 1952) around the age of 2. This phase of cognitive development lasts until about 6 or 7 years of age and is the phase of focus of this book. Children of this age can engage in symbolic thought but it is very inflexible. They can engage in elaborate symbolic play enacting complicated storylines, but they are often inflexible in the roles they assign: "No, David, you cannot wear the dress because boys don't wear dresses." or "No, you can't be the baby in the game because you don't have a baby at your house." Children are also very egocentric in their thinking. They know that things happen for reasons, but those reasons often have a very egocentric quality. For example, a child may say, "It's time for you to get off the swing now." This indicates that this child has a concept of turn-taking and that a turn on a swing is measured by the passing of time. However, when the child on the swing asks why, the child responds, "Because I want you to," and this indicates that although the child understands turn-taking, the reason he thinks it is his turn is very egocentric. Children in the preoperational stage of cognitive development have precausal ideas about causality. For instance, they say something such as, "It's raining because the grass needs water." They may also attribute animate qualities to inanimate objects. Consider 4-year-old Robert, when asked to describe his house drawing. "My house looks just like any kind of house. The color of it is kind of gray. It never falls down because it's too strong. It's strong enough to stay still." Children of this age often become confused between symbols and the objects they represent. Young children may become afraid of toy animals that look real and ferocious and will often avoid playing with them. They may approach the toy animal in a cautious way that looks like they think the toy animal will bite them. Thus, children in the preoperational phase of cognitive development will often appear frightened of something that is harmless. It is important for adults to understand these limitations in young children's thinking, especially if they are going to be helpful in talking with them about fears. In order to talk with a child and to get that child to talk back, an adult must be able to understand a situation from that child's point of view.

Finally, young children are able to focus on only one dimension at a time. They cannot conserve number, mass, and other variables. Their thinking is also not reversible. Therefore, they often are not able to understand and accept simple concepts, for example, that a child can be angry with a friend but still remain friends with that child. We often hear young children say to one another after they have had an argument, "I'm not your friend anymore and you cannot come to my birthday party." Adults certainly cannot change the way young children think, but they can introduce enough disequilibria in the child's thinking to encourage the use of more flexibility. It does not help for an adult to say, "That's not nice. Of course you will still be friends and she will come to your birthday party." Rather, it is more useful to begin to help the child to see more than one way to react when she is angry with her friend. An adult may say, "Oh, you are angry at her right now because she would not share her beenie babies with you. You really did have a good time with her earlier this morning. I'm sure you will feel better about it later, but right now you are angry and don't feel like being with her. It is better to tell her that you are angry at her because she did not share than to say she cannot come to your birthday party." These are just some comments to make. Certainly, one would not make all of these comments to a child at any one time.

Thus, it is important to understand the qualities of preoperational thinking in order to be able to talk with a young child in a meaningful way, and in order to encourage a child's verbalizations. It is important to talk with a child in a manner that is not condescending and that communicates to the child, "I am listening and I am interested in what you have to tell me." Children readily pick out adults who talk with them and not at them and know which ones will listen to them.

Language Development

There is a close connection between the development of thought and the development of language. Language also develops within a social context and depends on social development (Bates, 1976). Various theorists attribute importance to different factors in the development of language. The nativist view (Chomsky, 1976) stresses that children are preprogrammed and have an innate ability to acquire language. The behaviorists focus on the importance of the language environment. The infant and young child need appropriate language models and constant feedback as they attempt to communicate. Other theorists (Piaget, 1952; Vygotsky, 1962) viewed the development of language as a complex interaction between the child and the environment, which is influenced by both social and cognitive development. Both Piaget and Vygotsky believed that as children develop language, they actively build a symbol system, which helps them to understand the world. They differed in the way in which they viewed how language and thought interact with one another. Piaget believed that cognitive development led to the growth of language whereas Vygotsky viewed language as developing thought. A child's external speech is the first step in the development of thinking. Vygotsky's theory stresses the importance of communication with others as a major factor in the development of a child's language, which stimulates the development of thought. Vygotsky's theory views the important effect that an adult has on the development of language. His theory describes the importance of the zone of proximal development, which is present in interactions children have with adults. This zone is described as the "distance between the child's actual developmental level determined by independent problem solving and the level of potential development as determined through problem solving under adult guidance." This adult guidance is referred to as scaffolding. In order for the scaffolding to be effective, it must match the child's developmental level so the child is comfortable enough to use the guidance, which may present enough of a challenge to reach the next level in a particular area. For example, an adult whose goal is to provide an appropriate amount of scaffolding may engage in a conversation with a young child using various strategies. If the child asks a question about a particular topic, the adult may first ask a child, "Well, what do you think about that?" Once the adult knows what the child thinks, he can decide which ideas to confirm and which ones to extend and determine just how much information the child can assimilate during one conversation. Adults who do not typically provide scaffolding will not ask the child's thoughts on the matter, but will answer the question directly. In doing this, they have not figured out exactly what the child is asking, nor do they know what the child already knows about the particular topic. Even though the child in this situation may be satisfied with the answer, he has not had the opportunity to actively discuss and manipulate ideas in order to construct knowledge. Sometimes adults can ask young children open-ended questions. The children's responses are often filled with information, which adults in the scaffolding role can extend. Consider the various answers these 3- and 4-year-old children gave to a teacher's question, "What do you know about leaves?"

"The leaves fall from the trees and they always roll away."
"They do their jobs. They grow."
"They fall on the ground."

Samantha, Age 4, "Princess"

"The wind comes and blows them very fast and they roll across the grass. I can catch one of the leaves."

"Sometimes the leaves get into beautiful colors like a rainbow. They fall to the ground and I catch them, and when they stay up in the tree and they do their jobs and keep growing and growing and growing."

Clearly, these children already have a vast knowledge about leaves. The teacher can then take this information, which is meaningful to the children, and weave it into discussions about seasons, the life cycle of plants, weather, and an appreciation of the beauty of nature. A teacher can say, "You were talking about how the leaves get into beautiful colors like a rainbow. Let's find a book about leaves and find out how they do this."

Play and Development

One way we can get a view of the social, emotional, cognitive, and language worlds of children is to understand the development and use of play in young children. Play allows children to reveal their inner world, including their perceptions of important relationships, feelings, anxieties, wishes, and conflicts. It is very easy to observe young children at play in the classroom, on playgrounds, and in their own rooms. All children use play for a variety of reasons, and the quality of play varies from child to child. The following example of the play of a group of 4-year-old children illustrates some complicated play. These children did not just suddenly become good players. From early on, they were supported in developing interpersonal skills, a sense of playfulness, a sense of separateness, skills with materials, and play as a way to express themselves.

> The setting is the grassy, tree-filled spacious outdoor play yard of a day-care center. It is late in the fall; the sky is blue and sunny and there is a slight chill in the air. At promptly 11:00 A.M. the door bursts open. The four-year-old group dashes out into the play yard and begins to scatter to favorite swings, climbers, bikes, trees, etc. Suddenly, Libby, age $4\frac{1}{2}$, the leader and probably the most popular child in the group, falls to the ground and lies there immobile with arms stretched out to the side and eyes closed. Scott, Arthur, and David, all $4\frac{1}{2}$, spot her and yell, "Quick, Libby's dead!" Libby vigorously controls a smile from coming over her face and continues to lie immobile. Scott grabs a police hat and Arthur gets a fire hat. Both jump onto the nearest tricycles and begin a journey around trees and under bushes to Libby's rescue. David grabs the wagon, identifies it as the ambulance and follows Arthur and Scott. Along the way, they make contact with the rescue station and one another through their imaginary walkie talkies. Eric, age 3 years and 10 months, leaves his favorite swing and runs circles around Libby calling, "Teacher, Teacher!" in a high-pitched voice, and then repeats to himself, "Libby is not really hurt. She is just pretending," but he does not seem to be able to convince himself of this and begins to yell louder for teacher help and fights back tears. Scott, Arthur, and David appear on the scene and help Libby into the wagon. Scott calls the rescue station and says, "We're bringing her in." David begins to make siren noises and pulls the wagon toward the rescue station being built by some of the other children. Once at the rescue station, David announces, "I'm the doctor," and begins to examine Libby who is still lying quite still and limp. David completes his exam and sadly announces, "She's dead." Scott and Arthur begin to walk away. Libby smiles, jumps up, and begins to run. As she notices that Arthur, Scott, and David are pursuing her, she falls down and the story begins again.

It is clear from this example that the play of these children was important business and had different meanings and outcomes for all of the children involved. Clearly, they are all interested in playing out age-appropriate concerns of control, bodily intactness, and death. Eric struggles more than the others because he is younger, and his ability to distinguish between reality and fantasy is not as well developed and, thus, he at times believes Libby is really hurt. Such a play sequence allows one to realize that play has many definitions and functions, takes on different forms, and becomes elaborated and changed with maturation. It also is a wonderful example of how children often use repetition in play to master a difficult experience or concept.

It is agreed that play is important for the development of intellect, personality, and socialization. Research has found that play increases the flow of ideas, divergent thinking, representational abilities, intellectual abilities, social skills, and the development of imagination (Singer, 1972). Rogers and Sawyers (1990) outlined the ways in which play can contribute to the development of cognitive skills. Play allows children to practice new skills in a nonthreatening way and to consolidate something they have learned before. Children love to repeat skills in their play as a way to achieve mastery. Play enables children to manipulate objects and experience many things. Play "unites the mind, the body, and the spirit." Through play, children learn to symbolically represent their world. Because play is usually driven by the child, it allows for the development of a playful attitude, flexibility in problem solving, curiosity, persistence, and a general sense of relaxation around learning a new skill or concept. Ervin-Tripp (1991) found that play improves language and offers children the chance to dialog, solve conflicts, and share ideas. Children who play regularly obtain high scores on tests of creativity and imagination (Dansky, 1980). All of these benefits of play emphasize how important it is to support a child's use of play to enhance cognitive development.

Play and Cognition

Piaget (1962) studied children's play and described its many cognitive benefits. He described play as the child assimilating reality to the ego. This process is best described when observing an 18-month-old child at play.

> Eighteen-month-old Jonathan was playing with his toy farmhouse. He had set up a corral and was carefully placing each of the farm animals inside. He then gave each of the animals something to eat by placing troughs by groups of different animals. He made vigorous eating sounds for them, and then he tried to step inside the 3 by 6 inch corral so that he could also eat.

Jonathan was clearly assimilating reality to his ego in that he did not realize that he was any bigger than the little animals. Piaget also said that children use their play to experiment with their ideas about objects, events, people, and places. One can see this was happening in the rescue and hospital play of the children previously described. Children's play also supports the development of symbolic representation, which is necessary for the development of language and abstract thought. In general, play allows children to integrate, differentiate, and expand their understanding of the world. Play very much supports the growth of cognitive development. Consider Jonathan at 30 months, after hours of play with his little farm and other toys that encourage the use of symbolic play. He will not still be trying to step inside the little corral and his cognitive horizons will have expanded. He will have more complex ideas about his size in relation to his toys, and he will have developed ideas about classes of animals and places to eat.

Play and Social and Personality Development

Children's play also supports the development of personality and social–emotional well-being. Teachers view preschool children who spend more time in play as more socially adept than their peers who do not play as much (Burns & Brainerd, 1979; Connolly & Doyle, 1984). Clinical evidence has shown that play allows a child to assimilate a difficult experience (Harter, 1983) and that play can be a vehicle used by the child to express wishes and conflicts The cognitive benefits of play are that it organizes a child's thoughts. The emotional benefits are similar in that they help organize a child's personality by aiding in the resolution of conflicts, which allows development to progress (Biber, 1963). Erik Erikson (1964) aptly described play as "allowing a child to find refuge in the world of toys" and "allowing a child to hallucinate ego mastery half way between reality and fantasy." In other words, play allows a child to find outlets for complicated and conflicting emotions. According to Barbara Biber (1963), in a paper entitled "Play as a Growth Process," children who can use their play to find some relief experience growth in their development as people and develop richer personalities, which helps them to tolerate conflict and strong emotion. Those who cannot play or who use play in a repetitive and defensive manner often become inhibited in their play and their approach to themselves and their world. The following examples illustrate how young children use their play to be able to express and tolerate strong feelings and conflicts. The first example is of Brian, a normally developing child, and the second example is of Kevin, a child referred for therapy because of his phobia of tornadoes.

Three-year-old Brian loved to dress up in costumes that he would put together to be a Power Ranger, Batman, Superman, etc. The costumes were all very elaborate and required time and skill to put together. He often chose to play these games when his big grown-up uncles came to visit. He would dash around the room conquering many foes looking and feeling somewhat more potent in his cape than in his Osh Kosh overalls. After one of his many quests, he revealed his inner longing. He swaggered over to the table where his mother and aunt were sitting and said quite seriously and hopefully, "Mom, when I am 4 and I am a man, I will get a car." This superhero play allowed Brian to hold onto the wish of becoming a grown-up as big and strong as his uncles.

Kevin, age $4\frac{1}{2}$ was referred for therapy because he had a phobia of tornadoes. The phobia seemed to represent many things to him including fear of his out-of-control feelings, a wish for and a fear of engulfment by his mother and his mother's depression. When he began therapy, his play was very rigid and not useful to him. In other words, he was not able to use his play to find some relief from his anxieties. The play sequence would always be the same. The family would be in their house when suddenly a tornado would instantly destroy everyone and everything in its path. At first, the therapist explored the meaning of the tornado with him, but he could only go so far without becoming very anxious. The therapist then began to offer him some ideas about giving more adaptive endings to the stories. She introduced the idea of a storm cellar and then she and Kevin began to write tornado stories. These suggestions motivated him to learn about the weather. He then was able to use his intellectual abilities to gain some control of his feelings, which then allowed his play to become less inhibited and rigid. What eventually happened is that he became what Biber (1963) described as a successful player, that is, someone who could use his deep feelings in connection with his cognitive functioning to help elaborate his play to the point that it became a vehicle through which he could freely express himself and gain some insight into his inner world. Over time, Kevin became less inhibited. He no longer walked on his toes as if to take off like a tornado, and he no longer had a need to play tornado over and over again. His play turned to other interests and conflicts.

The Functions of Play

The descriptions in the previous section illustrate how play is a child's way of expressing how different events, people, and themselves are experienced and is a key to understanding the child's inner experience. There are at least seven distinct and separate functions that play has in the social and emotional world of young children. First, it allows children to repeat pleasurable experiences. Second, play helps children express feelings and master difficult situations. Third, it helps children learn about the world by trying on the roles of others. Fourth, play helps young children practice emerging social skills, such as making friends, joining groups, solving conflicts, and sharing ideas.

Fifth, play can often be cathartic and can serve as a tension releaser for young children. Sixth, play can help children assimilate an over-whelming experience by allowing them active control in their world of make-believe over something they have been a passive recipient of in their real world. And, finally, play can be a way in which children can express interpsychic and intraphysic conflict.

Many children use play to gain active control over something they have passively experienced. Children are always acting out such things as going to the doctor, being a parent going off to work, taking care of babies, etc. When children are overwhelmed by a situation, their play often becomes repetitive and reveals their experience and perception of a situation, which may be very different than what adults perceive of the reality. In these circumstances, play can reveal the powerful messages that children are trying to communicate. Con-sider the following clinical example, where a child is clearly trying to gain active control over some very difficult situations.

> Anna, age 4, was a child who had serious medical complications during her first 2 years of life. She had surgery for cancer when she was 5 months old, which left a very large scar on her stomach. She underwent chemotherapy for several months. At 14 months, she developed spinal meningitis and then seizures, and she had to be medicated. She was very anxious and confused about her medical history as no one had been clear with her about any of it, and she had never asked about the scar on her abdomen. She was an anxious child who managed her anxiety by oppositional behavior. She also spoke very quickly and very emphatically. She loved to carry an adult-size pocketbook in which she kept her makeup, which she sometimes would put on when she was feeling particularly anxious or vulnerable. The following play sequence illustrates how she was assimilating a difficult experience. It also gives us a sense of her relationship with her mother and of her anxiety and confusion about her illness.
>
> Anna picked up her pocketbook and baby in a very businesslike manner. She said quickly and firmly to the baby doll, "Baby, here is your medicine, so you will be good." Then she busied herself at the stove making dinner. She poured water from one pot to the next stirring vigorously and humming. She turned and said to her baby doll in a sing-song and sweet but hostile voice, "Hooneey, I'm fixing your dinner." She then sat the baby at the table, gave him a little sip of food and then said angrily, "No, you can't have any more food. You have to share." Later, the baby was taken to the doctor for a checkup and a blood test. The doctor was extremely rough with the baby and kept pushing him on the stomach and using a syringe to take blood from the stomach.

This clearly is a dramatic example of the way children use play to assimilate difficult experiences and express their worries and con-fusions. This one play sequence was enough to illustrate Anna's tremendous need to both explore her past and understand her anger and anxiety in a therapeutic setting.

Children also use their play to express conflict. The following example illustrates a child's use of play to express conflict.

> Robbie was 4 years old when he began therapy. He enjoyed making clay figures in his play. The main character was named Smoker. Smoker had a girlfriend whose name was Never Mind. In a particular play sequence, Smoker declares that he wants both Never Mind and a fancy jet. He is told by God that he cannot have both. The therapist suggests that he tell the story two ways. In the story where Smoker gets Never Mind to be his, the two clay figures stick together, become one lump of clay, and get hung up on a rock and are unable to get off. Robbie was unable to tell a story about Smoker getting a fancy jet.

This was a very complex story that continued for weeks. It contained different scenarios such as Smoker wanting to be the boss of the world, wanting a girlfriend but never finding one, and struggling with more powerful foes. It perhaps illustrated some of his conflicts about growing up, negotiating triangular relationships, and his desiring to be omnipotent.

Types of Play

There are many aspects of play; and there are many different kinds of play, which a child may use at home or school. Parten (1932) did extensive observations of children's play and classified it into four different categories. In unoccupied play, the child is not playing and is usually observing other children at play. In solitary play, the child plays alone and watches but does not enter other children's play. Solitary play is prevalent among 2- to 3-year-old children. Associative play involves some social interaction but little or no organization. Cooperative play involves interaction in a group with a sense of group identity and play, which is very well organized. This type of play is typical of older preschool children. The example of the outside hospital play is a wonderful example of cooperative play. Usually the most informative kind of play is the symbolic or dramatic play that has been described in the many examples given thus far, but children do not only engage in this kind of play. They also enjoy exploratory play, skill mastery play, construction play, and imitative play. The child who enjoys looking at and experimenting with all of the toys presented best describes exploratory play. Children who engage in skill mastery play enjoy throwing and catching balls, playing games, or mastering a climbing apparatus. Construction play takes place when children put together manipulative toys such as tinker toys or legos or build with unit blocks. Imitative play takes place when children imitate what another person is doing, for example, engaging in domestic mimicry such as pretending to cook, taking care of babies, and imitating superheroes seen on TV or in videos. The child who engages in these latter types of play as well as symbolic play can be best described as a robust player. Children who avoid engaging in symbolic play may do so to avoid the painful feelings or conflicts the symbolic play may create for them.

Development of Play

There is a progression that play follows from infancy through the preschool years. The group of children in day care whose play was previously described did not just become good players when they turned 3 and 4. They had been given opportunities to develop these skills through relationships and exposure to materials that support the development of play. The progression begins in infancy with play by oneself and also with a primary caregiver and progresses through the preschool years where play takes place in the world of toys and one's peers. When infants wake up from their neonatal phase, they quickly begin focusing on interactions with primary caregivers. It is through these interactions that babies acquire several abilities needed to play early games and pretend. Parent–child games, such as peek a boo, so big, patty cake, and others all lead to the development of playfulness, a play intent, and a make-believe attitude. If these qualities are not observed in the interaction between a parent and a baby, one would need to explore the quality of the parent–child relationship more closely to determine why this was not developing.

Toddlers who are successful players engage in beginning symbolic play and domestic mimicry. Through their play, they work on issues of impulse and bodily control, separation and loss, and individuation. These issues lead them to play games where they are constantly filling and dumping containers, thinking about what is inside and outside, and playing games of coming and going.

Preschool children develop increasingly complex play skills. Their symbolic play typically expresses concerns about triangular relationships and bodily intactness and power. They love to take on adult roles in their play and constantly use their play to resolve conflicts.

Children who play in nonclinical settings also engage in play that can be expressive of their ideas. Adults can observe children's play to determine what these thoughts and feelings may be. Repetitive themes in the play are often important to observe and follow. Additionally, disruptions in play may indicate that the content of the play has led to an increase in anxiety. Adults can make comments about children's play scenarios to get some information that may be useful in discussing difficult issues. For example, an adult may say, "I notice when you play that game with the dollhouse that the little girl is always getting lost. I wonder how that happens?" The child may respond verbally about this, choose to ignore the comment, or elaborate the play to express some ideas about the little girl's tendency to become lost. In either situation, the adult gains some more information about the child's experience.

Curry (1985) found in her studies of pretend play in day-care centers that pretend play was often absent in the classrooms because it was not given any recognition. She found that if make-believe play were supported even in a minimal way, however, the children became very engaged and busy in their play. Most normally developing children enjoy all kinds of play, but if the environment is set up to encourage symbolic play, they will often be drawn to that (Curry, 1985). An analysis of the child's symbolic play is necessary to decide whether the child uses play to assimilate a difficult experience, express feelings, or express conflict. This information is useful to adults who are engaged by children to discuss difficult subjects. Children will often use play for all of the aforementioned functions. Examples from clinical play sessions help to illustrate these functions.

Play That Allows a Child to Assimilate a Difficult Experience

Mark, 4 years of age, had been referred for evaluation because of difficulty with toilet training, sleeping through the night, and becoming independent in an age-appropriate way. He was a premature twin. His twin sister died in the newborn unit when she was 2 months old. Mark remained in the newborn unit until he was 3 months old. He had never been directly told that he had had a twin sister; however, he must have assimilated some information about this by hearing adult conversations in his family. During the diagnostic play session, he repeated three times a story about two babies who were walking home. They were both shot by the police because they were not listening. The babies were then taken to the hospital and had to spend a very long time there. After a long hospitalization, Mark turned to the clinician and said, "This is very important. I am afraid she did not make it."

Clearly through this play, Mark was trying to assimilate his confusions about his early history. In addition, he expressed concerns about the consequences of the expression of aggression and strivings for independence.

Play That Allows a Child to Express Feelings

A clinical play session allows a clinician to determine whether a child's affective expression is age-appropriate and adaptive. One is interested in the kinds of feelings a child expresses both in the play themes and outwardly when he or she is playing. These feelings and behaviors can also be observed in children's play outside clinical settings. Do children express a range of feelings? What is the level of intensity of these feelings? How does the child modulate these feelings? The following example illustrates a child who was struggling with the expression and control of his strong angry feelings.

William, 5 years of age, plays with the toy family in his play session. The boy in the family is named Joe. Joe has a special talent. He can snap his fingers and get everything that he wants, even things that he is not usually allowed. Joe's sister, Casey, enters the scene. She begins to wreck everything in the house. Then the mother and father tell her she cannot go to the circus because she wrecked the house. Joe happily goes along with his family to the circus while Casey has to stay home alone. William says, "Casey will be so mad that she will blow up." Clearly this play sequence would allow adults to explore issues of strong feelings and sibling relationships.

Play That Allows a Child to Express Conflict

Five-year-old Samantha was interested in playing with Star Wars figures. The main character in her play was Princess Leia. She was portrayed as very independent and strong minded. She only wanted to marry Yoda (the wise old man), even though all of the other men tried to woo her into marrying them. She, however, only wanted Yoda, and Yoda supposedly wanted to marry her, but they never did get together in the play sequence.

From Samantha's history, she seemed to be dealing with age-appropriate Oedipal conflicts (Freud, 1946), such as becoming more

Etana, Age 4, "Alligator and Monkey," (from "The Alligator Song")

separate from her parents while at the same time competing with her mother to win her father's exclusive love. She was using her play to express and cope with these conflicts.

Toys and Symbolic Play

Thus, children really do engage in play to express feelings, resolve conflict, and assimilate a difficult experience. This kind of play can be encouraged in all young children and can serve as a springboard for discussion of difficult issues. Simple open-ended toys, which invite fantasy play, are the best materials to choose when trying to set up a play environment for a child. An attractive set up of the toys is almost like setting a stage or a table for a special meal. It is inviting to the child and communicates that the adults are interested in the child's play and the ideas and feelings connected with it. Some of the basic toys include: a simple doll house with furniture and people (preferably families), rubber animal families (both wild and domestic), plastecine or play dough, paper and markers or crayons, baby dolls with dishes and bottles, wooden blocks, and puppets. It is important to avoid using the toys that are more commercial (i.e., from videos and television shows), as these tend to inhibit the child's play, which becomes a repetition of the shows and contains very little of the child's inner world.

Conclusion

Thus, by the time children are in the preschool years, they have developed rapidly in the social, emotional, cognitive, and language areas. They are well equipped to talk about and play out a variety of difficult issues, and they are interested in exploring these topics. Most of the time, they are more interested in and comfortable with exploring these issues than adults are. Adults will be able to speak with them about these topics if they remember that children of this age are very concrete and egocentric in their thinking, are struggling with issues of dependence and independence and separation and control, are curious about the unknown, and often already have their own ideas or theories about difficult topics which need to be understood by adults before adults begin to offer answers to children's difficult questions.

Let's start with the dark and see what we have learned from children.

3

"I Am Afraid the Dark Will Keep Me Night Night."

Helping Children to Talk about Fears

Children's Fears

Two-year-old Jonathan was having a hard time getting to sleep. He began to cry and asked for both his mom and dad. After trying to soothe him, find his blanket, and tuck him in, his parents asked him, "What's wrong?" He replied, "I am afraid of the dark." At that his parents brought him into the living room and turned on the lights. He continued to cry, seemed really frightened, and repeated "I am afraid of the dark." When his parents asked him, "What is it about the dark that makes you afraid?" he replied, "I am afraid that the dark will keep me night night. I am afraid that the dark won't go away." Jonathan's parents, who were ready to say, "You don't have to be afraid of the dark," were speechless for a moment as they pondered the gravity of what he just said. What a frightening thought for anyone, much less a 2-year-old who is working so hard to hold onto a view of himself as separate and independent. To lose that self to the dark is, indeed, a frightening and overwhelming thought. We are often so quick to say to children like Jonathan, "Oh, don't be silly. There is nothing in the dark to be afraid of. It can't hurt you." If it seemed silly to Jonathan to be afraid of the dark, he would not be afraid of it. We have to continue to remind ourselves as adults that although children's fears may seem irrational or unimportant to us, they are very real and frightening to the children who have them. Our own fears may seem very irrational to our spouses or friends, but we do not feel understood or calmed down when they say, "You should not worry about that." Let's think a bit about fear in general.

We usually become frightened or anxious when we feel we cannot control or understand something. In fact, over the history of our species it has been, at times, essential for parents to teach their offspring to be fearful in order to avoid dangerous or life-threatening situations. Even though many of us say to children, "Don't be afraid," I think we would all agree that it is important to fear certain things. We don't want to encourage children to be completely fearless and, thus, be unable to protect themselves in dangerous situations. In fact, we want children to have a healthy balance of fearfulness and an excitement for trying new things and taking risks. Even so, children as well as adults have different styles and tolerance levels for how they achieve this balance. Some people need constant excitement and thrive on doing the scariest things. Four-year-old Jason once told an adult friend that he liked the TV show, "Dungeons and Dragons." She asked him, "What do you like about Dungeons and Dragons?" He replied quickly, "I like when it is over because then it is not scary anymore." Others are more cautious and avoid that which frightens them. These styles usually develop through a complex interaction between the individual and his or her environment.

Whereas adults have developed their own set of fears and strategies for dealing with them, children are just starting off and develop fears from a variety of sources. There are also certain fears connected with specific developmental phases and stages, which are described shortly. Children are helped to develop specific strategies for coping with their fears and anxieties. They can teach us a lot about their fears if we support their ability to talk about and describe their fears. What they tell us about their fears can help us to determine how much their fears are interfering with their development and adjustment. What they tell us provides us with some information to use so we can help them confront and cope with their fears. We deceive ourselves if our goal is to completely take away their fears or to question ourselves, "What did we do wrong as parents to make our child afraid of the dark? Doesn't she know we always keep her safe? Are these fears a sign that she is going to have serious emotional problems?" Our goal is really to acknowledge that our children may have something to say about their fears that may help us to help them cope in a more adaptive way.

Three-year-old Matthew was having trouble falling asleep and called for his mother. He pointed to his favorite stuffed animal and tearfully said "Puppy is afraid of the dark." His mother asked, "Why do you think he might be afraid of the dark?" Matthew replied, "He is afraid of having night-mirrors." His mother asked, "Can you tell him the dark won't hurt him?" "He's not listening," Matthew replied, "He wants the light on so he won't have night-mirrors."

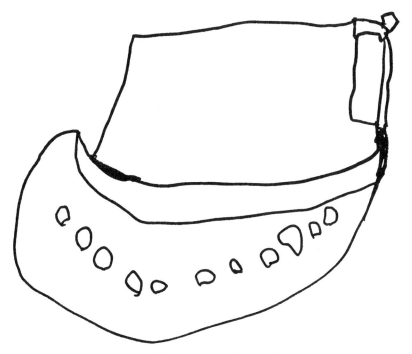

Matthew, Age 4, "Fire Boat"

Thus, although we can speculate why Matthew or "Puppy" is afraid of the dark, we won't really know why. We do know, however, that this particular evening, Matthew felt listened to and could, therefore, find a way to cope with his fear and be able to fall asleep.

Learning Fear

Where do fears of such things as the dark, monsters, bad guys, and witches come from? We know that fears can come from a variety of sources. We know that children are always watching and trying to emulate adults. They can easily learn to fear something from an adult. All parents are concerned about their children's safety and know it is their responsibility to keep their children safe. Parents have different ways of convincing themselves that they may be ensuring their children's safety. For example, parents can give messages to children about their own fears, their ideas about their children's competencies, and safety while they are supervising an activity as simple as a child's exploration of a piece of challenging playground equipment. One parent might continually say, "Don't go any higher. You might fall and get hurt." Some parents might even go to the extreme and say, "If you fall I may have to take you to the hospital." Another parent might sit away from the piece of equipment and occasionally say, "Be careful, don't fall" or "See if you can go faster or higher." Still another parent may stand by a child and say things like, "Look how you can climb. Hold on with both hands. Let me know if I can help. That looks like high enough today. Maybe tomorrow you can try to climb higher. I can't let you go that high because it is not safe." This latter parent is more likely to have a child who uses a reasonable amount of caution when trying new or challenging activities. Children who experience the limits of the first parent are likely to be overly cautious and fearful. Some children who are always told to be careful can actually appear careless and reckless and they often do not develop a personal sense of what the safety limits are or a sense of realistic confidence in their own abilities and limitations.

Children can learn fear from sources other than their parents. They can have truly frightening experiences, such as a hospitalization, an accident, witnessing a frightening event, or watching a frightening television show or movie. Some children are temperamentally more fearful than others. Usually, parents can easily accept their children's fear if they know their children are unusually sensitive or if they have had a difficult experience. It becomes more challenging for parents when children's fears seem most irrational. Young children think differently than adults, and these differences may cause a child to feel fearful during everyday, usual events.

Young Children and Fear—Cognitive Influences

What are some of these differences in thinking? First of all, young children are very egocentric in the way they view the world. The world revolves around them and they have a difficult time seeing another person's point of view. They often cannot understand another person's feelings. They will become upset if their parents are upset. Because they are so egocentric, children may think that they did something to upset their parents. Although this is sometimes the reality, there are many times when a parent's upset feelings have nothing to do with the children. A parent may not be openly upset or fearful, but many times children can sense this upset or fear and react to it. One day, 4-year-old Matthew's mom was preoccupied and quiet thinking about an upsetting event at work. Matthew asked her anxiously, "Why do you have a mad face? Are you mad at me?" This egocentricity can also affect how children interpret everyday events. A group of 4-year-olds was having snack at day care when they heard a siren. Tony anxiously turned to the teacher and asked, "Are the cops coming to arrest us?" After the teacher reassured them, the siren continued and the children began a conversation about police cars, ambulances, and fire engines. When the conversation turned to fires, John anxiously said, "I heard on TV a fireman got shot. He wasn't my uncle." These two examples of egocentric thinking certainly indicate how easy it can be for a child to become frightened by everyday events that might not appear potentially frightening to adults.

Besides being egocentric in their thinking, young children engage in quite a bit of magical thinking. They tend to think that saying or thinking something will make it happen. A wonderful example of magical thinking occurred one day during a kindergarten meeting. Peter, one of the aggressive children in the group, had had a difficult morning. He struggled to join a group building with blocks. Once he accomplished being accepted into the group, he proceeded to knock over a very elaborate building. The other children were furious with him and told him he could no longer play. He was angry and sad and stomped out of the block corner. When he was at lunch, he proclaimed that he was so angry that he might blow up all of the children's houses. One of the boys who had most vigorously refused to play with him said in reply, "But you don't know where I live." Imagine if a child thinks that thoughts, words, or feelings can make things happen. Wouldn't they become frightened by some of their thoughts such as, "I wish that baby had never been born." or "I'm gonna crash down the school." or "I hate when you go to work." It is becoming clear that children's fears, although seemingly benign to adults, need to be taken seriously.

In addition to having a tendency toward egocentric and magical thinking, young children are also just learning to distinguish between reality and fantasy (Freud, 1965; Piaget, 1952). They can easily lose their grasp on reality especially if they are watching a scary show or playing a game that is frightening. Children may need to repeat to themselves not to be frightened of a particular event. Recall 3½-year-old Eric, from the previous chapter, who was watching some 4-year-olds pretend play, which consisted of one child falling down and pretending to be dead and the other children rescuing her and taking her to the hospital. Eric watched from afar, paced in a circle, and anxiously called "teacher teacher" while repeating to himself, "Libby is not really dead. She is just pretending." Eric obviously was repeating words he had heard from adults but probably also needed some reassurance about his reality testing.

Fears Associated with Developmental Phases

Fears of Infancy

The young child's tendency toward egocentric and magical thinking, and some confusion between reality and fantasy are not the only sources from which fears can develop. There are well-documented fears that are considered developmental in nature that are often made worse by the young child's way of thinking about his or her outside world. The major fear connected to infancy is the fear of the loss of the protective and nurturing environment and, in later infancy, the fear of the strange (Freud, 1946, 1965). These fears find symbolic expression in fears of dark, noises, strangers, and being alone (Freud, 1946, 1965).

Toddler Fears

During toddlerhood, fears are connected to the developmental struggles the toddler faces with separation, the development of independence, and the development of sense of self. The fears include fear of the loss of love and approval, the loss of the self, and the loss of the parent. Remember when we talked about 2-year-old Jonathan. He was frightened of the dark because he was afraid that at night he would lose himself in the dark. It is feelings of loneliness and helplessness that toddlers work hard to avoid (Freud, 1946, 1965). These particular fears find symbolic expression in fear of punishment, rejection, and desertion as well as in fears of earthquakes, thunderstorms, and death (Freud, 1946, 1965).

Preschool Fears

Preschoolers who become keenly aware of the bodily differences between the sexes develop fears about bodily integrity and intactness. These particular fears find symbolic expression in fear of operations, doctors, dentists, illness, poverty, robbers, witches, ghosts, etc. (Freud, 1946, 1965).

They also begin to fear the loss of their parents' love as they negotiate the triangular relationship between themselves and their parents. Thus, we know that young children's development in several areas, especially the cognitive and social–emotional areas, influence the

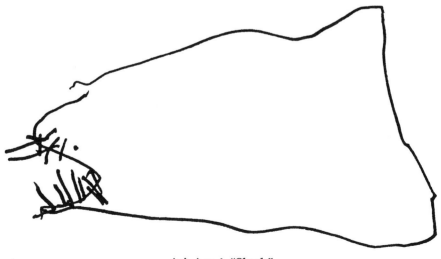

Ari, Age 4, "Shark"

development of particular fears. We also hopefully have an appreciation of what some of these fears mean to children, especially the fears that seem simple and unrealistic to us. With this knowledge we can then begin to think about children's fears and develop some reasonable coping strategies to help them deal with these fears.

Helping Children to Cope with Fears

As we begin to think about how to help our children deal with and talk about their fears, we have to remind ourselves that we do not want and cannot try to ensure that our children never experience pain and fear. Besides being impossible, this would not have been developmentally supportive even if it were possible. Many parents think (with good intentions) that they need to protect their children from certain anxiety-producing information. The parents of a child who had had a complicated medical history and who needed a psychological evaluation because of behavior problems were reluctant to tell their child she was coming to see Dr. Jones. They thought their child would become too anxious and would not cooperate with the evaluation. Dr. Jones encouraged them to tell the child and see what kinds of questions she would ask about it. The child, of course, was full of questions and then was delighted to come see a doctor who did not give blood tests or shots, put in IVs, etc. Clearly, these parents were able to let their child lead the way through her questions and avoid even more anxiety when she eventually met Dr. Jones. Other parents assume that the way to help children master anxious feelings is to give them lots of information about the thing that is most frightening to them. For example, a $3\frac{1}{2}$-year-old who was struggling with issues of power, size, and aggression was both frightened and fascinated by the news of the bombing in the Gulf War. His parents encouraged him to watch the news with them as much as possible. They encouraged him to ask questions and answered them as accurately as possible. They overloaded him with so much information that he could describe all of the details of the most recent bombing. This little boy seemed overwhelmed by the amount of the information he was given. He became very aggressive and controlling. His parents began to realize they had overloaded him with information and were not allaying his anxiety but, rather, fueling it when they overheard him telling a friend about the most recent bombing. The child told his friend that the bombings were really far away and said they were happening in the town next to his. Thus, when the child heard loud noises, he more than once asked his parents if they were bombs. Certainly, far away meant something different to this 3-year-old than it did to his parents. The boy's anxiety abated somewhat when his parents were very concrete about how far away the bombings really were and when they waited until he asked questions before giving him information.

Both sets of parents in the aforementioned examples had very good intentions. They knew that children sometimes need to be protected from overwhelming events and that they need to have some information to understand certain things and events. Neither set of parents, however, was letting the child lead the way.

In the first example, the child was not initially given the opportunity to react to the fact that she was going to meet another doctor. The second child was given too much information, and his parents were not responding to his overwhelmed reactions to this information. We often are much wiser parents in retrospect, after we have seen how our child reacts to a particular fear. There are some guidelines that we can follow that can help us to support our children's attempts to cope with fears. The suggestions come somewhere in between the extreme examples and cover five areas.

How Much Information?

First, it is important to give children information. When children ask questions, it is important to answer them as honestly as possible. You do not want to give too many details at first, because you want to give the child permission to talk about it, and you also want to be certain what the child is really asking. For example, the little boy's fascination with the bombings could have been explored a bit more before he was exposed to so much information. His questions and anxieties could have been very different from what the adults thought they were. One way adults dealt with the Gulf war was to gather as much information as possible. Doing this provided a sense of control over the completely chaotic and unbelievable situation. This amount of information and intensity, however, was too much for the little boy. This point leads us to our second guideline.

Children's Responses to Questions about Fears

Second, once we give children information, we want to watch them react to it, and encourage them to talk and ask more questions. The questions they have may be very different than the ones we think they have. For example, the little boy we discussed was more concerned with how close the bombs were to him than with the details of the bombings. The details appeared to make him more anxious and overwhelmed and distracted him from asking about what frightened him the most: "Am I going to get hurt by the bombs? Are they coming to my house?" The best way to encourage children to talk and ask more questions is to say things such as, "After you think about this for a while you may have more questions." Parents often ask, "What if he asks a question I either cannot answer or am unsure how to answer?" It is always fine to say to a child, "That is a good (or a difficult) question. I need to think about it for a while before I can answer it for you. I will let you know." Sometimes engaging the child in conversation about the question can be illuminating.

Making Connections between Feelings and Behavior

Third, we help children talk about and cope with their fears by making some connections between their feelings and behavior. There are certain behaviors that indicate to us that children are feeling stressed by fear. These behaviors include disruption in sleeping or eating, increased activity or aggression, withdrawn or distant behavior, and extreme reactions to normal events. For example, the 3-year-old boy who was worried about the bombs became more active and aggressive. A helpful connection might be, "You are running around and seem very excited. I wonder if you are feeling worried about something?" or "You really are fighting and hitting a lot. I wonder if thinking about those bombs is making you feel scared or excited?" Sometimes children are unable to talk directly about their fears and may too quickly answer the questions, "No, I'm not scared. I'm not scared of anything." In these situations, it is often helpful to make connections for the children in more indirect ways, such as through the characters in their play. I have observed many children enjoying a game of talking to a shadow called "Woof Woof," made by a flashlight and a parent's hand while relaxing before stories at bedtime.

One night, a 4-year-old girl carried on a long conversation with "Woof Woof" about the impending birth of her new sibling. This little girl had been extremely oppositional with her mother but had not accepted connections that she was upset or worried about how the sibling's birth would affect her. Woof Woof suggested that the baby might be really noisy when he or she cries. The little girl agreed and animatedly described all the things this baby might do to annoy her.

While she chattered on, she relaxed and the next day her fights began to subside. For many nights after that, she continued to ask for Woof Woof before her bedtime stories.

Fears and Stages of Development

For our fourth guideline, as we are helping children understand and cope with their fears, we need to ask ourselves, "What does their particular fear mean at their developmental stage?" Remember, in general, infants fear the loss of the protective and nurturing environment. Toddlers generally fear the loss of love and approval, and the loss of self and the parent. Preschoolers have fears about bodily integrity and intactness as well as fears of losing their parents' love. Just because a preschooler has made it to age 4 does not mean that he or she no longer has toddler or infant fears. Aspects of all of these phases of development are woven into children's personalities.

Recently, I was told about a little boy, 5 years old, who was going on his first overnight trip on a boat. He was both excited and anxious about the impending trip. He took delight in seeing pictures of the boat and measuring his backyard to compare its size to that of the boat. He drew pictures of the boat. He had denied he was afraid of the boat until one night he asked, "Do we have to sleep in our life jackets?" When his parents replied, "no," he then asked, "Well what if the boat sinks? Who will help the kids put on their life jackets?" Clearly this little boy's healthy fears of the impending trip can be connected to several phases of development including fear of the strange, loss of self, loss of parent, and concerns about power and potency. Knowing these various phases can help us empathize with the child's fear as well as give the child strategies for mastering these fears and, ultimately, experiencing new events in a positive way.

Idiosyncratic Meaning of Fears

The fifth and final guideline we need to follow when trying to help children cope with and master their fears is to pay attention to the idiosyncratic meanings children give to their fears. These meanings are as different as children are. It is important to be aware of the origins of these fears, respect their meanings, and make connections for children. For example, Matthew, age 2, would become very fearful when he thought his food was too hot. He would begin to cry and ask his mother for help. He had spilled a cup of hot tea on himself as a younger toddler and had a third-degree burn on his chest. He gradually became more comfortable with the temperature of his food as his parents made the distinction for him between the food they prepared for him and the unfortunate accident of getting into tea that was prepared for someone else.

Conclusion

In closing this chapter about helping children to talk about their fears, it is important to repeat the general themes. Fear is an inevitable human emotion that can be useful in development. There are typical fears associated with the various developmental phases. Children express their fears through their behavior, play, and words. If children are responded to when they communicate (in any of these ways) their fears to adults, they will in general feel more comfortable and tell adults more about how they can be helpful. One of the most difficult tasks for parents is to face the inability of being able to allay children's fears completely. Even when we talk with children and they freely ask us for help, there are times when children have to face and live with the fear alone.

Five-year-old Matthew was doing some beach and cave exploring with three friends and his mother. At one point, he became paralyzed with fear thinking he had climbed too high. Although his mother was right by his side and was ensuring his safety, he began to shake and cry and said loudly, "I wish Santa were here." Although his mother was devastated that he did not feel comforted by her presence and ability to keep him safe, she appreciated that he was able to articulate the level of his fear. Later, when he had returned safely home, he talked about how high he had climbed. He admitted it was very scary, but he was proud and excited that he had made such an accomplishment. He realized on some level that, even in the presence of his mother, he had to face the fear alone.

4 "I Feel Like Killing My Mommy."

Dealing with Angry, Aggressive, and Rageful Feelings

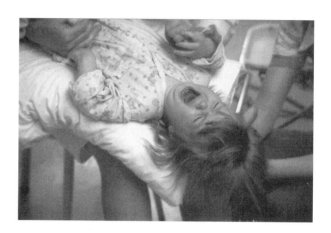

Children's Expression of Anger and Aggression

Four-year-old Jonathan was shopping with his mother at his favorite toy store. They were buying a birthday present for his friend. Jonathan's mother explained to him that he could buy a small inexpensive toy for himself. He decided ahead of time that he would choose a small car he had seen a few weeks before. He chose to buy his friend a large fire truck. As he and his mother were ready to buy the toys, Jonathan asked her if he could also get a big fire truck. She said, "no," explaining that they had agreed he would get an inexpensive toy. He pleaded a few times and then begrudgingly bought his small car. He walked quietly to the car. He flung himself into his seat and muttered as he fought back tears, "I feel like killing my mommy." His mother said, "I know you are really angry at me. I am sorry you are disappointed." She left it at that and Jonathan slowly began to explore his new car.

> On reading this mother's response you may have many strong reactions, such as the following:
>
> How could a child have such a violent thought?
>
> Why did Jonathan's mother not admonish him for speaking so violently?
>
> Do children get these violent ideas from watching too much TV?

Whatever the question, people usually react to such a statement made by either an adult or child with a sense of concern. This points to the fact that we all have difficulty expressing anger and rage. Many of us would rather admit that we were feeling frightened than that we were feeling angry. We often do not know what to do when we are angry and we feel especially uncomfortable when we are angry with a child. If we are experiencing anger and do not know how to talk about or even acknowledge anger, how can we help our children to do this?

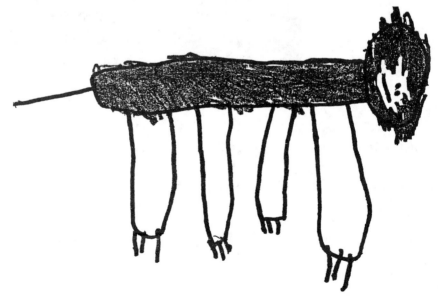

Jonathan, Age 4, "Lion"

We need to remind our children, and maybe also the more vulnerable side of ourselves, that expressing angry thoughts does not necessarily mean that we are going to act on them. In order to begin to think about how we can help children to talk about anger and express it appropriately, let's first focus on what we know about the development of aggressive feelings and behavior and the important and normal role such feelings and behavior play in development.

Developmental Aspects of Aggression

Channeling Aggression

Aggression and aggressive energy are essential ingredients for progressive development (Freud, 1946, 1965). When channeled and expressed appropriately, aggression allows for self-preservation and the development of the ability to assert oneself appropriately (Provence et al., 1977). It allows a child to develop a sense of separateness and independence (Mahler, 1975). Aggression is also an essential energy for learning. Channeled aggressive energy allows a child to be curious, persistent, questioning, competitive, and motivated to master skills and challenges and to solve problems. If one considers the tremendous amount of growth and learning that takes place during the preschool years, it is not surprising that there is a normal upsurge in aggressive energy during this phase of development. The development of the ability to channel and express aggression takes time and patience. Some children have a harder time with this than others. But, in general, it is appropriate to expect that children become more able to use words than actions to express their anger as they develop through the preschool years. There is often an intermediary step where children use their words to express anger, but they also give into the impulse to hit and hurt. Eisenberg and colleagues (1998) found that, over time, children's abilities to regulate emotion shift from depending on external controls (e.g., parents or teachers) to using internal controls. In addition, they increasingly use better cognitive and coping strategies when regulating emotions and are able to modulate emotional arousal. Eventually they are able to enter situations and relationships that minimize negative emotional reactions. Young children do not have the ability to use all of these skills and need adults and maturation to achieve inner controls when experiencing feelings of anger and aggression.

Development of Inner Controls. It is clear that aggression is a necessary ingredient for development. It allows for survival, self-protection, and learning. One only has to observe a group of children in order to realize that feelings of love and hate are naturally intermingled and that one tends to turn aggressive and negative feelings toward loved ones throughout one's life. The development of the ability to manage aggressive impulses goes through a series of stages. In normal development, these impulses are brought under control by loving impulses or the investment in relationships with others (Freud, 1946, 1965). The child's sense of trust in himself and others is the basis on which these relationships are formed (Erikson, 1950). The deeper the trust and the more stable the relationship, the more likely and quickly children are to develop inner controls and more appropriate ways of expressing and channeling aggressive energy. As with the growth of any important capacity, the development of inner controls is a process that takes time. A 5-year-old is less likely to have a temper tantrum when frustrated than a 2-year-old, but 5-year-olds do sometimes lose control of themselves and either tantrum or hurt someone.

Adults as Models of Self-Control. How do children best learn to develop inner controls and express their anger appropriately? As mentioned before, they first need to have developed a basic sense of trust in themselves and others. It is the investment in preserving this relationship with others that helps children learn to inhibit the urge to hit or hurt when angry. Over time, it becomes more important to them to have their parents' acceptance, love, and approval than to give into their impulse to lose control. Children also depend on adults to be role models for how to express anger and frustration. If adults regularly lose control around children, then children in their identification with adults will emulate out-of-control behavior. If adults express their anger verbally or, after losing control, make connections to their behavior and express how they might have behaved differently, children can then begin to use their words to express intense feelings of anger and/or frustration. In addition to being role models, adults also need to have age-appropriate, clear, and consistent expectations about the expression of anger and aggression. If adults give the message that the expression of any kind of anger is bad or shameful, children may quickly conform to these expectations but may not necessarily internalize the ability to control themselves. They may also turn the anger against themselves and become depressed and withdrawn. On the other hand, if no rules or limits are set, children may continue to lose control and push until limits are set for them. These children do not develop inner controls and may be seen as having serious behavior problems.

Recent research by Strassberg, Dodge, Pettit, and Bates (1994) indicates a relationship between the type of punishment used at home and kindergarten children's aggression toward their peers. Children who are regularly spanked are three times more likely to retaliate aggressively if they feel wronged in an interaction with a peer. Children who are violently punished engage in a significant amount of bullying aggression. Katz (1999) found that children's abilities to control negative emotions varied according to the ways their parents reacted to the expression of strong affect. "Emotion Dismissing Parents" typically ignore, deny, or try to change emotions that are negative. "Emotion Coaching Parents" help children to label feelings, allow children to express negative emotions, and teach them how to cope with negative affects. The children of "Emotion Coaching Parents" are more able to soothe themselves when they are out of control and control negative affects than are the children of "Emotion Dismissing Parents." In addition, children of "Emotion Coaching Parents" develop fewer behavior problems than the children of "Emotion Dismissing Parents." Thus, allowing children to experience and express strong emotions, such as anger, helps them to eventually develop inner controls.

Toddlers and Aggression

The development of inner controls depends on external limits and expectations and the quality of the child's relationships. Development of inner controls also depends on the internal state and developmental level of the child. As previously mentioned, the child's experience and expression of aggressive impulses go through a series of stages during the preschool years. During the toddler years, between the ages of 2 and 3, there is a normal upsurge in aggressive energy (Freud, 1965; Furman, 1990; Parens, 1989). This aggressive energy is necessary to fuel the tremendous amount of development in the language, motor, cognitive, and social–emotional areas. This is a time when children are defining themselves as separate and independent individuals. In order to do this, they learn to assert themselves and push away from their primary caregivers. This task requires aggressive energy. They also become easily frustrated as they learn the world does not always work the way they want it to. Because language is not always

Cara, Age 5, "The Sun"

well developed at age 2, children express their frustration through tantrums and losing control of themselves physically.

Preschoolers and Aggression

As children grow older, they begin to develop the ability to express themselves verbally. This development is gradual and does not mean that children are able to completely express their anger or frustration verbally. A child may scream at another child, "Don't take my block!" while at the same time he tries to aggressively pull the block away. This may be considered an aggressive act, but the child is still trying to use his words to express anger. With the development of the ability to express themselves verbally, children are likely to say things that are violent or hateful, such as, "I'm gonna blow up your house." or "I feel like killing you." In situations like this, adults need to remind themselves that saying something does not mean the child will act on it or become a violent adult. Recently, it has been very hard for adults to do this because of the stories in the news of shootings and bombings at high schools and elementary schools. It is not helpful for a teacher to immediately send a child home who says something like, "I'm gonna blow up your house." Nor is a teacher being helpful if he or she says, "That is a bad thing to say."

Helping Children to Express Anger

There are ways that adults can respond to children's comments in order to help them better articulate and expand their feelings. First, it is often useful to say, "You are really angry at me, and I think you must feel really out of control." Second, it can be reassuring to a child who is feeling so out of control to hear an adult say, "Well, I will not let you hurt me. I can stop you if you cannot stop yourself." This needs to be said in a way that is nonthreatening and not in a way that might be challenging; otherwise, the child may become frightened and escalate the threats. Children are often worried if they feel so out of control that adults are capable of similar feelings, and children sometimes persist in expressing their angry thoughts in an attempt to provoke an out-of-control reaction from the adult. Knowing that children fear a reaction from adults can help adults know how to respond when children are out of control. Once, while teaching a class of 4-year-olds, I was setting a limit for Louis, who insisted on climbing onto the block shelf and jumping onto the floor. After I stopped him for about the fourth time, he looked at me anxiously and asked, "Well, aren't you going to hurt me?" I was surprised and said, "No, Louis, I am not going to hurt you, but I am angry that you are not listening to me." He immediately looked relieved, and he stopped testing the limits.

Third, adults may not know why a child is so angry, and they may need to help the child explore beyond the present situation in order to determine why he or she is reacting so strongly. It may be useful to say, "I know you are angry that you have to wait for your turn, but I wonder if you are also angry about something else." Such statements can help children reflect on their feelings and maybe understand their intense reactions. Adults can also make connections for children, although one has to be careful not to attribute reasons to feelings without a certain amount of confidence. Saying something such as, "I think you are still mad at Jesse because he said you could not come to his birthday party yesterday, and now he is the one having the turn," might be helpful. The child may respond with, "Yeah, well he cannot come to my party." The best way for an adult to respond to this is to say something such as, "I know you are really upset right now, and you will have your turn soon. Maybe you will get the first turn tomorrow."

Most children enter the preschool years with fairly well-developed verbal skills. They are able to identify and express a variety of feelings. They have developed a sense of separateness and independence and are gradually giving up the idea that they can control everything in their world. They are beginning to think about being grown up and can sometimes become anxious and frustrated when they do not have the same capacities and privileges as adults. One child, just about 4 years old, said to his mother one day after he had played an aggressive game of chase with his uncles, "When I am 4 and I am a man, I am going to get a car." Preschoolers are also learning to negotiate triangular relationships, the primary one being the relationship they have with their mother and father (Freud, 1932). The form that aggressive behavior usually takes on during the preschool years is that of aggressive exhibitionism and the expression of a competitive, dominating attitude (Freud, 1965; Provence et al., 1977). Imagine yourself on a playground with 4-year-olds. It won't be long before you see games of chase (good guys vs. bad guys) and hear things such as, "I'm not your friend anymore." or "Our fort is bigger than yours." or "Let's get the bad guys." or "But why can't we play with guns? They are fancy and exciting and they protect you. We're only playing big kid games."

Even though older preschoolers have better developed verbal skills and can usually use their words to express aggressive feelings or impulses, they sometimes do lose this ability, lose control, and resort to having a tantrum or losing physical control by hitting, kicking, throwing, or biting. We cannot expect preschoolers to always be in control, but we can remind them of the importance of using words when expressing their feelings. Although we can intellectually understand the reasons for aggressive behavior in young children, we cannot always remember these reasons when we are dealing with aggressive children, especially children who are testing our limits. Children who are being aggressive or defiant can cause an adult to feel angry and negative, and in some cases, to react in an aggressive, competitive, and sadistic manner. In other words, such behavior in children may make us feel that we want to get in the sandbox and fling some sand ourselves. It is times like this that we can be models for the children and put our thoughts and feelings into words. In order to be a good role model for expressing strong negative feelings such as anger, adults need to acknowledge their own anger in appropriate ways. Sometimes adults think it is best to hide their anger when they are around children. Children, however, can see through teeth that are clenched into a smile and experience an adult's anger even if the adult is trying to remain composed. This is more confusing for a child because the facial expression and demeanor of the adult do not match the underlying affect. There are many things that young children do that may make adults feel irritated or angry. These include whiney behavior, persistent testing of the limits, prolonged temper tantrums, physical aggression toward adults or other children, and obstinate refusal to do something. One of the most important things an adult can do is to acknowledge and accept the angry reaction in themselves. If they feel they might lose control, adults need to let another adult take over for a while. If there is not another adult nearby, they need to walk away and take a break. Deep breaths and counting to ten often help. Adults may need to say things such as, "I can't stay here right now because I am angry with you and not really feeling in control. I am going to ask (person's name) to help you get in control while I control my angry feelings. Then you and I can talk." At other times adults may need to say, "It really makes me angry when you do not listen to me." or "I don't like it when you keep grabbing that puzzle from Sarah. I wonder how I can help you to stop doing that."

Conclusion

When adults try to help children talk about their anger, they need to be willing to hear strong words and know that young children are not capable of acting on words such as, "I am going to blow up your house." The important job for the adult is to react to the child's strong feeling of anger and acknowledge how overwhelming it can feel and how out of control the child must feel. Adults can point out to children that sometimes their choice of words such as hate, kill, and blow up might be a bit too strong and might make the child feel even more afraid. At the same time, they need to acknowledge that a feeling strong enough for them to use such words must be frightening. An adult could say to a child, "You have a big, angry feeling right now. I think I can help you with that. When you say to me, 'I feel like killing my mommy,' I know you are really angry with me. I know you really wish you could have that fire truck. I will not change my mind even if you get very, very angry." This kind of interaction shows the child that people react to the things they say and have their own affective reaction, which may be different from the child's. It also models for the child how to talk about strong affective experiences without losing control.

5 "When You Die, Can I Live in Your House?"

Children's Reactions to Death, Separation, and Loss

Children's Curiosity about Death

Recently, there were two events at local day-care centers that made for interesting observations about how differently adults and children approach talking and thinking about death. Adults can sometimes work very hard to avoid talking about death with children because they do not want to upset them. In one center, the pet goldfish died. The adults quickly replaced the dead goldfish and told the children who noticed the original was gone that something was wrong with the water and the fish became ill. They, however, did not mention that the fish had died. The children did not ask any further questions and there was a missed opportunity to find out what the children's questions and thoughts about death were. The teachers were really giving the message that questions were not welcome.

The contrasting observation took place at another day-care center and illustrates how children very naturally explore the concept of death in their spontaneous play.

Patrick, Gregory, and Hillary were on the playground building a structure with plastic milk crates. Patrick and Gregory announced the structure was heaven, which was for dead people. Hillary said that she was a dead person and a baby. Patrick said she could go into heaven because she was dead, but she could not go in right away because God was there. Gregory had a rock and a stick, which he called a magic rock and key, that had to be in heaven during their play. Gregory saw Hillary lying in the sandbox with her eyes closed. He said that Hillary was dead. He picked her up and began walking her to "heaven." Hillary kept her eyes mostly closed except for a small squint as she made her way to "heaven." Once she arrived, heaven became a hospital. She was put in a bed for dead people. There were nurses who took care of dead people all day and all night. Hillary needed to stay in heaven for 18 days. After the time passed, Hillary turned into a baby and the play changed its focus to babies.

These examples illustrate that young children do encounter death in their lives. In most cases, the death is usually that of a pet or a grandparent. In unusual cases, young children have to cope with the death of a parent or sibling. Children do think about death and they have some concepts about it that are different from adult concepts. Adults are, in general, uncomfortable speaking about death with children because they do not want to upset them.

How, then, can adults become more comfortable with talking to children about death? It is useful to understand young children's cognitive understanding of death and how to distinguish curiosity and anxiety about the concept. It is also useful to understand how young children are influenced by their developmental status, especially in the area of how they cope with issues of separation, independence, and loss. Finally, as has been stressed throughout this book, just listening to what children have to say about death teaches us a significant amount about what is on their minds. It is also important to go beyond the surface of what they are saying to gain a true picture of their thoughts. For example, 4-year-old Jasmine's mother died very recently. An adult friend observed Jasmine at the funeral and commented that she did not think Jasmine really understood what had happened and what was going on. She said this because after the funeral was over and friends and family were gathered for a reception, Jasmine kept saying she wanted to go home and watch "Land Before Time." What this friend missed was how profound Jasmine's comment actually was. This particular movie is about a dinosaur whose mother has died. The dinosaur feels lonely and frightened as he searches for his mother, ever struggling with the need to realize he will never find her and feeling completely lost and alone. Jasmine was communicating the depth of her sorrow to those who could understand the metaphor she was using.

Children's Comments and Questions about Death

When children are encouraged to speak and ask questions about death, they say some interesting things. Because they are so egocentric, they are usually worried about what will happen to them if a parent dies. Their most immediate concern is who will take care of them. Four-year-old Matthew once asked his mother, "What will happen to me if you die?" His mother replied, "Daddy will take care of you." Not satisfied, he then asked, "Well, what if Daddy dies, too? Can I still live in your house?" His mother replied, "No, if Daddy dies, too, you will have to go live with Aunt Ginny and Uncle Richard." Matthew then said happily, "Yeah, then I get to live on a farm." At that point, Matthew had no further questions. What he really wanted to know was who would take care of him if both of his parents died, and he was satisfied once he received the necessary information. Clearly, Matthew's questions reflected the egocentric thinking of a 4-year-old. In addition, this discussion about death did not fuel any particular fears in Matthew. He did not become worried that his parents were about to die. In fact, he stopped worrying about it because he knew that someone would take care of him if his parents were to die. At that moment, this was all he needed to know.

Children do sometimes worry about death and need to ask quite a few repetitive questions until they feel comfortable with the answers. Five-year-old Justin overheard adults talking about someone getting killed by a volcanic eruption because he went back for his camera. For 20 minutes, Justin grilled his parents about this story. This is a sampling of some of his questions.

"What happened?"
"Why did he go back for his camera?"
"How did he die?"
"Did he miss his mommy when he died?"
"Did his mommy cry?"

Each of these questions is very difficult to answer, and again reflects the egocentricity of young children. Justin assumed the dying person would feel the same way he would in a similar situation. It was his mommy he was thinking about. Justin's anxiety was reflected in the rapid repetition of his questions. He also felt better when he himself could say that if he were in a similar situation he would not run to get his camera. Instead, he would run to safety. This more adaptive solution gave him a better sense of control over the overwhelming story. When Justin began asking questions, the adults tried to distract him by saying they did not really know the details, and they tried to get him to talk about something else. To Justin's credit, the adults did begin to engage in conversation about this event with him. After this discussion, Justin began to feel less anxious, and was able to move onto another topic of conversation.

Children's Concepts of Death

Young children often do not understand the permanence of death. In addition, they do not understand that when someone dies, all bodily functions cease. Sarah asked her mother after her grandmother's funeral, "How can grandma breathe under the ground?" Another little girl, who was playing on the playground shortly after her grandfather's death, was loading up the baby carriage to go to heaven to see grandpa. Consider the following conversation between a 4-year-old and a 5-year-old.

"My grandma died. Yeah she's right up there."
"I don't see anything up in the sky. I just see clouds."

Later, the 4-year-old, Nicole, asked her mother, "What is this sky business? How did Jenny's grandma get up there?" Her mother then explained death to her, telling her that Jenny's grandma had been very old and had become very sick and that she died. She told her that some people believed that when people died their spirits or souls go to a place called heaven and that people thought this place was in the sky. Nicole's response to this explanation was to say, "Well, I don't ever want to go up there," and then she went on with her play. Her mother's response to this comment was to say that she had a very long time to live and many things to do before she had to worry about dying. Although adults cannot deny that death does or will happen, they can respond to children in realistic ways so children feel that their questions are answered, that they may ask more questions if they need to, and that it is okay to express anxiety about this complex and overwhelming concept.

Helping Children to Talk about Death

Children's questions reveal their struggle with and curiosity about the concept of death. Adults wonder whether children are irreparably harmed from talking about death. Children need to know it is okay to ask questions. If adults avoid their questions, children will think they are talking about something bad. This will inhibit their curiosity and make children feel more anxious about death. Recently, at a local nursery school, a child's mother died after a long illness. The director wrote a letter to the parents in the class telling them of the news. She also told them she would be telling the children about the death in school the next day. Some of the parents called the director and asked her if she really thought it was a good idea to tell the children and whether she thought it would upset them too much. The director very appropriately said that, yes, she was going to speak with them because they always talk about things that happen to the children in the class. Even though it was a painful topic, she felt the children needed to talk about it and be helped to process such a difficult event.

Death as It Relates to Issues of Separation/Individuation

One of the reasons preschool children seem so interested and curious about death is that they are struggling with issues of separation and loss at their stage of development. They are working on the process of becoming individuals with a sense of separateness and independence. The process, which continues on through adolescence and adulthood, requires children to deal with issues of separation and loss.

The 6- to 9-month-old infant who begins to recognize a difference between familiar and unfamiliar faces must give up the idea that she and her primary caregivers live in a placid, symbiotic state. The toddler who strives for autonomy (Erikson, 1950; Mahler, 1975) must relinquish the idea that either he or his parents are omnipotent. The preschooler who goes off to day care for the first time must cope with feelings of anger and sadness over missing his parents during the day and must reconcile these feelings with the excitement he feels over engaging in a growth-producing school experience. The adolescent who vigorously fights for her independence must really move out on her own and no longer expect or wish that her parents can solve her problems. All of these forward movements in development require that children experience some loss. It is these losses that sometimes cause children to think and wonder about death. The most challenging kinds of loss that both children and parents must learn to cope with are those that require children to separate from their parents. Both children and parents can experience separation anxiety when coping with these losses. It is how we help children to understand and cope with these normal anxieties that affects the role separation anxiety plays in their development. This also affects the ways in which children are then able to express questions about death. In order to help children both understand and cope with their own separation anxieties and questions about death, adults helping them need to understand their own separation experiences and anxieties.

Preschool Children's Developmental Reactions to Loss.   When one observes the amount of energy young children expend understanding and coping with separation and working to achieve independence, it is easy to see why preschoolers begin to show an interest in death and ask questions about it. Although independence is their goal, the actual achievement of it can be exhilarating, overwhelming, and frightening. In order to achieve independence, children need to give up or lose certain aspects of their babyhood. It is this loss that can stir up feelings of both anger and sadness. Some of these feelings can be very intense and are most often directed toward children's parents. Thus, the ambivalence becomes confusing to the child.

Young children begin to ask questions about death for many reasons. First, because they are more independent, they are more aware of events of nature and the lifecycle of both plants and animals. They naturally become curious about the human lifecycle and begin to ask questions about the abstract concept of death. They ask repetitive questions because their minds are very concrete, thus making it difficult for them to accommodate their schemata to such abstract concepts. Second, because young children experience feelings of loss both as they achieve their independence and when they make daily separations, they do think and worry about the permanent loss of people. Third, children experience ambivalence over the loss of the dependency of babyhood. They do sometimes long for the easy days of babyhood, and when they become challenged by their independence, they expect their parents to be omnipotent and able to resolve their conflicts. When they realize their parents are not all-powerful, they have intense reactions, which are often characterized by anger and sadness. These feelings can seem uncontrollable to children and they worry whether their powerful feelings could get out of control and cause some danger to those they love. It is due to a young child's egocentricity and tendency to engage in magical thinking (i.e., if I think or feel something bad, bad things will happen) that they do worry about the danger of powerful feelings. It is these feelings that set in motion a child's anxiety about loss both in the day-to-day sense and in the final sense. Consider the 4-year-old who talks about her father who has moved out of the house because her parents are getting a divorce. She said, "My Daddy does not want me anymore. My Daddy doesn't want to live." Right away she experiences thoughts of loss and rejection, which then become connected to death in the little girl's mind. Clearly, she has articulated in this very short but powerful statement what is on her mind and gives adults the opportunity to explore her feelings and anxieties with her.

Thus, it is clear that children do have the ability to think and talk about death and that they are interested in expanding their horizons about the concept. Preschool children are in the preoperational phase (Piaget, 1952) of cognitive development. This level of thought is very concrete and egocentric. Children tend to use magical thinking. Because of their particular way of making sense of their world, young children consider the definition of death in ways that do not completely grasp the permanence, universality, and nonfunctionality of death. This ability to grasp the complete concept of death comes around 7 years of age (Speece & Brent, 1984).

Children and Death

Young children think that death is reversible. They think that the person or animal that died will come back to life either in some magical way or after some time has passed. This is clear in the earlier examples that described the child who loaded up the baby carriage to go visit her grandfather in heaven, the child who asked when her grandma (who had passed away) would wake up, and the child who said about her recently deceased grandmother, "Grandma will come back in April because that's when my birthday is." It can often be painful for adults to hear children talk like this because in many ways what the children believe and think is often similar to what the adults are wishing for. They, therefore, think they should not be talking to children about death because they really do not understand and cannot grasp the concept. Although children understand death on their level of thinking, they still need to experience thinking about death to expand their understanding of it and, ultimately, to have an understanding of it that is both mature and consistent with their culture and beliefs.

A young child's view of death is also confused by the fact that they do not completely understand the nonfunctionality of death (i.e., when a person dies all bodily functions of a person stop). Although children can acknowledge that they know a dead person cannot move or talk, they often think the person's brain continues to work after death. Children say things like, "Grandma thinks about me." One 4-year-old said to her mother after her grandmother's burial, "How can grandma breathe under there?" This question indicated that this child still did not completely grasp the nonfunctionality of death, but she was asking the question she needed to ask to further develop her conception of death.

Young children do not at first understand the universality of death. They do not think about their own death or the death of their loved ones until they experience the death of a pet or a grandparent, or they hear about death on the news or know someone who has died. When they begin to understand this concept, they ask many questions about their own death and the death of their loved ones. These are the questions that make adults most uncomfortable and lead them to feel uncertain about how to respond. In general, the advice is to find out exactly what the child is asking. Then it is always important to give the child an honest answer even if it feels uncomfortable. A more specific discussion of this topic follows in the next section.

Factors That Influence Children's Understanding of Death. Young children's understanding of death is not only influenced by their cognitive capacities but also by some environmental and cultural influences, such as religion and exposure to death in their lives. For example, children who come from families that practice religions that have a strong belief in the afterlife often have difficulty developing an understanding that death means a total cessation of bodily functions. Such children also tend to understand death's universality and permanence more slowly than other children. In contrast, Schonfeld and Smilansky (1989) found that Israeli Jewish children had a more advanced understanding of the permanence and universality of death because of the experiences they had had with war. It is clear from this data that the task presented to those who want to help children understand and talk about death is one that requires them to understand developmental, religious, and cultural influences on a child's growing understanding of this topic. In addition, adults need to know that discussing death with children will not fuel their anxiety. On the contrary, it has been found that as children increase their cognitive understanding of death, they are able to manage and express their anxiety, instead of being overwhelmed by it (Essa & Murray, 1994).

Responding to Children's Questions.   Now that we understand how and when children develop a mature concept of death, the questions, "How can we help children ask their questions?" and "How do we respond to these questions?" remain. There are several factors that influence the way in which we help children to talk about death.

Know What the Child Is Asking.   First of all, it is important to make sure you know what the child is asking or what kind of curiosity or anxiety is pushing the question. It is, therefore, a good idea to first see what the child is thinking or asking before you answer. For example, a child may ask his mother, "Mommy, are you going to die?" Of course, the mother needs to answer in the affirmative, but before she does this she needs to find out more about the child's question. For example, the mother might say something such as, "Yes, everybody dies someday. I am wondering what made you think about my dying." It may be as simple as a child worrying his mother might die because she has been sick in bed with a bad flu and the child might think her death is imminent because he has learned that people often die when they are sick. If the mother asks the child why he is asking the question, the child could say, "Well, you are sick and grandma died after she was sick." It is also important to try to figure out why the child is asking questions about death at that particular time. It is helpful to think about what has been going on in the child's life that may motivate the asking of such questions. For example, 5-year-old Jonathan began asking his parents questions about death when an au pair arrived to live with his family for a year. She was very homesick for the first few days and he was aware of this. He could not imagine being away from his own mom and dad for so long and to him it would be like having his parents die. Of course, it was very painful for his au pair to hear these questions because she was so sad about being away from her own parents. He stopped asking the questions once the adults made it clear that his au pair could, indeed, speak to and write her parents and even look forward to seeing them when she went home.

Be Aware of the Child's Ability to Cope with Separation Issues. A second factor that influences the way in which questions are addressed depends on the child's ability to cope with feelings of separation anxiety. As is seen from the aforementioned example, Jonathan's questions were motivated by his own concerns about separation, and what he wanted to hear was not so much focused on death, but really reassurance that his babysitter would someday be reunited with her parents. Thus, it is important in answering the child's question to know whether he is asking about the concept of death or having concerns about some recent separations that he is having difficulty dealing with.

The Adult's Comfort in Talking about Death. A third factor that influences the way in which a child's questions about death are answered has to do with the comfort level of the adult who is answering these questions. Many adults feel uncomfortable answering questions about death. Recall the example earlier in the chapter where the teachers did not mention that the fish had died. It is not unusual for adults to often avoid using the words death or dying when they are talking with young children. Clearly, the questions they ask about death are difficult and can lead to levels of discomfort because there really is not an answer that can completely allay both the child and the adult's anxiety. When a child does ask a question about death that the adult feels he cannot comfortably answer at the moment, a good strategy is to ask the child what he or she thinks is the answer to the question. Then, if the adult continues to feel uncomfortable, he or she can say something such as, "That is a very good and thoughtful question. I need some time to think about my answer and I will let you know about it later today." Once an adult says this, it is important to follow up with the child so the child does not receive the message that difficult questions cannot be answered and that the adult will not answer the question. It will not be long before children who experience this will no longer ask direct questions about death. This may, in fact, make them more anxious as they try to answer their own questions and find themselves unable to do so. They may also answer their questions using their own cognitive strategies, which rely on magical thinking and egocentricity. These children will be the ones who insist they can go see their grandma in heaven or that their grandfather is having trouble breathing in his grave. Such thoughts can lead to increased anxiety, and nobody wants to be left alone with such thoughts. Adults would not want their children to face these answers alone and, therefore, it becomes essential for adults to find ways to be comfortable in both fielding and honestly answering children's questions about death.

Children Inevitably Talk about Death.   A final factor that influences the ways in which young children talk about death is adults' ability to acknowledge that they cannot protect children from thinking and talking about death. Children have a natural curiosity, and they want to know everything about their world. Wanting to know about death is just as natural as wanting to know about birth, how plants grow, or what clouds are. More than any other time, adults may be deceptive with children when they ask about death because they have this idea that children are always supposed to be happy and never think about concepts that overwhelm them. The fact is that children need to ask and talk about all concepts in order to refine and develop their ideas and their fund of information. It is when they wrestle with difficult concepts that they experience states of disequilibria (Piaget, 1952), which then motivates them to learn more and accommodate their cognitive structures to better understand an idea. If they cannot move from states of equilibrium to disequilibria in their thinking, then their ideas about particular phenomena remain unchanged and undeveloped. They also do not develop strategies for coping with concepts, which makes them anxious and uncomfortable.

Discussing the Death of a Classroom Pet.   Considering all of these factors allows us to revisit the day-care center where the fish mysteriously disappeared because the water was bad. No one used the word "died" with the children nor thought about how the death of the fish could be handled in order to stimulate discussion about the death of the fish and to develop an understanding of the children's concepts of death. First of all, it would have been helpful for the children if they had been able to see the dead fish before it was taken away. It really is all right for children to discover that the fish is lying on top of the water and not moving. Such an experience would easily generate a discussion about the observable characteristics of death. Children and teachers could discuss together that the fish is no longer moving, breathing, or eating. This would also allow children to ask why the fish had died. If, indeed, it was the water, then teachers could explain about ph levels of water and the danger of certain kinds of bacteria and the need to have the appropriate temperature in order for fish to survive. It would be useful for children to be involved in the disposal of the fish. Some classes will bury a classroom pet in the play yard and even have a memorial service and make a grave marker.

If teachers have a discussion with the children about how they want to remember the fish, they will have lots of ideas. The children's response depends on their experience with death and memorial services and the teacher's comfort level with the discussion. The death of a classroom pet may stimulate play about death. Again, this is children's healthy way of trying to assimilate an experience they cannot comprehend. Teachers have available to them many picture books about death that they can put in the reading corner of the classroom. In fact, it is often useful for a teacher to follow up a discussion of the pet's death with the reading of one of these books. One of the classics is *The Dead Bird,* by Margaret Wise Brown. Teachers should also wait a while before they buy another fish for the classroom because children need to have some time to continue discussing the loss of their fish. Some children may lose interest quickly whereas others may want to discuss it for weeks.

It is often interesting to try to figure out why particular children remain interested in the event after others have stopped talking about it. A simple statement to the child who continues to ask questions, such as, "Gee, you are still really wondering and thinking about how and why our fish died. I guess we need to talk about it some more," gives the child permission to continue asking questions. It is possible that some children ask these questions because they recently experienced a death of a pet or a relative or they are anticipating an impending death. They may also have their own issues of separation that the death of the fish intensified. The important message teachers need to communicate to these children is that it is all right to continue the discussion and that they will be available to discuss questions with them. A small number of children may continue to ask repetitive questions in an obsessive way a month or more after the event. With these children, it is important to say, "You are still really thinking about our fish dying. That happened such a long time ago. I wonder if you have some other questions about it that you haven't asked. I wonder what else you may be thinking or worrying about." Some children may be concerned that the water they drink or swim in may be bad and cause them to die. Others may be thinking that they may have done something to the fish water to make it bad. We may not know this unless the children are able to articulate their questions or concerns. Thus, again, it is essential to make sure that we communicate to the children that we are interested in their thoughts and questions even long after a particular event has occurred.

Discussing the Death of Relatives.   Discussing the death of a classroom pet can make adults feel uncomfortable, but they feel even more uncomfortable when they need to discuss the impending death or the death of a child's relative. Many times, when children are talking about or playing out the concept of death, they are not trying to assimilate the death of a loved one. When children experience a death in their family, adults often feel unsure of what to say to them and how to say it. They also do not know whether they should warn a child of an impending death of a relative.

The typical young child is most likely to experience the death of a grandparent. Some children have to cope with the death of a parent and others have to cope with the sudden death of a parent. All of these children need to receive an explanation of their relative's death. Although the experience of each kind of loss is different, there are some general guidelines to follow when talking with children.

Being Honest When Talking about Death.   First and foremost, it is essential to always be honest with children. They need to be given enough information in order to be able to ask questions and experience and express their feelings; however, it is important not to overwhelm them with details they might not understand. For example, a parent may say, "Grandma died today. You know she has been very sick with cancer and the doctors could not do anything else to make her better. The grown-ups are feeling very sad and we keep thinking about how much we are going to miss Grandma. I know you will also feel sad. You may have some questions about Grandma dying, and you need to know you can always ask those questions even if you think mommy is too sad to talk about it." In this example, the child has been given the necessary information, that her grandmother died from cancer and that her death will cause those who loved her to be very sad and to miss her. She has also been assured that whatever questions she needs to ask will be answered.

Providing Children Opportunities to Ask Questions.   Adults also need to provide some openings for children to ask questions. For example, when telling of a grandparent's death a parent may say, "You may wonder why the doctors could not make Grandma better." Finally, the information needs to be given to children in a developmentally appropriate way. The information given to children needs to be given as concretely as possible because young children understand their worlds in very concrete ways. For example, if a child asks, "Can I talk to Grandma?" an adult needs to say, "When people die, their bodies do not work anymore. Their hearts do not beat, they cannot talk, and they cannot think, but you can think about Grandma in your head and think about things you wish you could say to her." When adults talk with children about death, they also need to remember that children are very egocentric in their thinking. They often worry that bad things happen because of something they thought or something they did. They may not be able to directly ask about this worry so adults need to watch them and determine whether this is something they are worried about. Sometimes, if a child is testing the limits more than usual or continually asks why the grandparent died, he or she may be trying to ask if he or she was a cause of the grandparent's death. Adults then need to say to children something such as, "You know Grandma died because it was her time to die. She had a very long life and loved you very much. You did not do anything to make Grandma die." Children may need to hear this reassurance many times before they are comfortable.

Many parents will wonder whether they should take their young child to see a dying relative in the hospital. The main benefit to doing this is that it gives a child the opportunity to say goodbye. The difficulty is that children can become concerned if the relative is hooked up to IVs and various machines. For this reason, it is important to prepare the child for what he or she might see. It can be useful to say something such as, "Grandma has a tube in her arm, which is putting medicine into her body so she will not hurt. She may also have a tube in her mouth, which is helping her breathe. You may also hear some beeps from these machines. Even though she is connected to all of these machines, she will be happy to see you. We will only stay for a little bit because Grandma is tired, but you might have questions about what you see there and it's fine to ask your questions. You may also have more questions after we get home, and you need to let me know what they are." Parents can make their own decisions about whether to take a young child to the hospital. If they decide to go ahead with it, they need to be prepared to answer children's questions, remembering that it is natural for children to have these questions and that the goal of the visit is to find a way to say goodbye.

The Death of a Parent.   It becomes more overwhelming for adults to talk with young children about the death of a parent. If it is the surviving parent talking with a child, then that parent is in the midst of dealing with his or her own grief and may not always be available to the child and may not be able to answer questions or comfort the child. If a child's parent has died after a long illness, then the child should be helped to anticipate the death. Adults need to say things to the child such as, "Mommy's cancer is getting worse and the medicine is no longer keeping her well. The doctor says she will die soon." The child may ask, "When will she die?" Adults need to respond, "I really do not know but I can let you know when the time is near. The important thing for us to do right now is to spend time with mommy and the doctors will make sure she is comfortable." Adults also need to explain their own grief and despair to their children, "I have been feeling pretty sad and worried since mommy died. I know I have been crying a lot and you might worry whether I am going to be all right." It is enough to say this and then wait for the child's questions. Parents may also need to explain their shifting feelings, especially the anger that is present in the grieving process. Children often misunderstand the surviving parent's anger and sadness; they think it is meant for them. A parent needs to be able to say to a young child, "I guess I have also been acting pretty angry since daddy died. I have been feeling angry because I think it's unfair that daddy died. I didn't want him to die and I couldn't do anything about it." Again, young children will feel relieved that the anger is not meant for them and may also feel that they have permission to ask why she could not stop daddy from dying. If the surviving parent can reflect the complicated feelings that grieving entails, then the child can begin to make sense out of his or her affective reactions.

Finally, a young child who has lost a parent worries if the surviving parent will be all right or may also die in an untimely fashion. Children may not be able to ask such a question, so often the parent needs to say, "You might be worried that I am going to get sick like daddy was, but the doctor tells me I am very healthy. I am going to work hard to keep myself healthy so I can take care of you." Some children will persist and want to know who will take care of them if the surviving parent dies, and the parent needs to be able to describe the plan. All of this is extremely difficult in the midst of losing a spouse, but a parent's willingness to talk with his or her child about the process allows for mutual healing.

Sudden Parent Death. If a child's parent dies suddenly, there is no way to anticipate such a tragedy and everyone feels and reacts to the shock. Words obviously do not bring back the dead parent but they do give the child some way of understanding what has happened. It is useful for the child to hear just how shocked and upset the adults are. An adult who has suddenly lost a spouse probably needs some time to absorb the shock; therefore, the other important adults in the young child's life may initially need to be the ones to speak with the child and to be available to answer his or her questions. The child who has lost a parent in a sudden way has the same feelings as a child who has lost a parent after a long illness, only the former child may feel more intense worry over who will take care of him or her. There is often nothing to do to appease this worry until the surviving parent recovers from the shock other than for the adults to reassure the child that the rawness of the wound will soon subside for both the child and the adults. Adults can also help children build and maintain their memories of their deceased parent through pictures and a journal. These concrete reminders, although painful at times, are important for everyone to have.

Talking about a Parent's Suicide. Usually, when a parent of a young child has died, it occurs because of an accident or a sudden illness. Sometimes it occurs because of a suicide. Parents, in general, are very uncomfortable about talking with young children about death when it occurs after an illness, but they feel they have to protect children from knowing that a parent committed suicide. Children do need to know how their parent died. Even if they are lied to when there has been a suicide, they will know there is a secret they cannot know; therefore, they will not be able to ask the questions they so desperately need to ask and might not understand the surviving parent's guilt and anger. Suicide like any other difficult concept can be described to children in a sensitive and developmentally appropriate way so that they can work to understand the reason their parent died and ask the questions they so desperately need to ask. One 4-year-old who was coping with the suicide of her father said to a friend at school, "My mommy says suicide is when you don't want to live anymore. Why doesn't my daddy want me anymore?" Imagine if this little girl had not been given the appropriate information about her father's death and could not ask such a vital question. When adults talk with children about suicide, it is important to stress that it often occurs because of a mental illness that the doctors had been unable to make any better. They probably need to be told how the parent died, but they do not need to know a lot of details, just enough so they can ask their questions and let us know what they are thinking. For example, "Daddy has been very sad lately. Having such big sad feelings has been like having a very serious sickness. He worked hard with the doctors to feel and get better, but nothing was working. He decided his sadness was so big and strong he did not want to live anymore and he put a rope around his neck and pulled tight until he could no longer breathe and killed himself. This is called committing suicide. You may have lots of questions about this and it is important to talk to me about them. Even the adults are having a very difficult time understanding why daddy did this. It is important to remember that daddy did not do this because of something you did or said. He did it because he was very, very sick in his brain." This explanation is detailed enough yet simple enough to allow a child to begin to assimilate his or her parent's death. Because such tragic losses need to be constantly worked and reworked through at each developmental phase, it is essential that children receive the appropriate information from the beginning.

The Role of the Teacher.   What is the role of preschool or day-care teachers in helping children to talk about death? They are often the adults who are present when groups of children are playing out death or when they are gathered in a meeting group and a child says something such as, "My mommy says my grandma is going to die soon." They need to be aware of the different developmental levels of the children in the group as well as their particular life circumstances that may be driving their play or motivating their questions or comments. They need to be able to work closely with parents as they are observing play and hearing what children are asking or saying about death. Let's recall the example from an outdoor play sequence in the 4-year-old group at the day-care center where Libby played dead, and all of the children were organizing her rescue. Remember that Eric anxiously watched the play sequence from his swing and called to the teacher in a high-pitched voice, "Teacher, teacher, quick, Libby's dead." Then he is heard repeating to himself, "Libby is not really dead. She is just pretending."

This play clearly indicates that these children are thinking about death. Their thoughts are embedded in a typical game of chase, but they are also working on understanding a doctor's role in a caring for a dying patient, the bodily manifestations of death, and affective reactions to death. None of the children involved in this particular play scenario had experienced any recent death of a relative. Eric, however, who was anxiously watching from afar, had just experienced the death of his grandmother. The teachers were aware of this and when they observed his anxious reaction to the play, they were able to speak with him about his grandmother, and he was able to ask for reassurance that Libby was really okay.

Teachers and Parents Together.   When teachers observe that children are thinking about and playing out death, they need to react to the children's interests, as they typically do. They work to help the children think about how they would enhance their play. They also try to extend what children know about a particular topic by finding appropriate books and by answering their questions. If a child in the group is dealing with either an imminent or a recent loss of a relative, then teachers need to work closely with the parents to understand what kind of information the child has been given and the ways in which this information can be extended. Parents will often rely on teachers to help them plan how to tell children about a death of a relative. Many times teachers need to gently lead the way. Parents often want to be instinctively vague and protect their children from having to experience emotional pain or to struggle with confusing and difficult concepts. Parents may be so overwhelmed by their own grief that they do not know what or how to say something. They are looking for advice from the teacher. The teacher and the parent(s) need to work together to determine how the information will be shared both with the children at school and with the parents of the other children. Usually a letter is sent home to describe what has happened and summarizes the information that has been discussed at school.

Many teachers and parents wonder whether the child who has experienced the loss should be present when the group discusses the death. Often times the child who has experienced the loss is out of school for a while immediately after his or her relative has died, therefore, the child's absence needs to be explained to the other children. Thus, the child who has experienced the loss will probably not be present during the initial discussion. When the child returns, however, his or her return needs to be acknowledged. The teachers can do this when they greet the child on return. They can say something such as, "I am really glad to see you again. I know things have been really difficult for you and your family. It is a very sad time when someone you love dies." Teachers may also need to help the other children to tell the returning child how glad they are to see him or her. Sometimes teachers can speak for other children while they are standing with them. They can say, "I know Sarah has missed you and has been worried about you. She is sad for you because your grandmother died. I know she is glad you are back." This kind of comment gives a model to children. It is a model that indicates that talking with someone who has experienced a loss can be like any other conversation in which empathy is expressed and gives children some appropriate words to use when doing so. If the topic of the death comes up in a group discussion, then the teachers need to make sure that the child who has experienced the death is comfortable with a group discussion. The teacher may say to the child, "Is it all right with you if we talk about this right now?" If it is not all right then the teacher needs to find another time to discuss the topic with the children who are asking the questions.

Thus, teachers need to watch and listen and be willing to address the questions children ask about death. They need to engage in conversations with parents to describe what the children are saying and to support them in speaking with their children about death when their questions occur. They will meet resistance with some parents. It is important to work with and understand the resistance, but at the same time it is important to educate and support parents.

Conclusion

This chapter has explored how children naturally think about and play out death. Their ability to develop concepts about death is limited by their cognitive abilities. They are very curious about death and wonder about it just as they wonder about why there are clouds in the sky or why the stars shine at night. They will continue to ask questions and talk about death if adults are able to answer their questions in a comfortable and informative way. As with any question children ask, adults do not need to answer right away; they may tell the children they are asking some very hard questions which require them to have time to think before they can answer them. Adults always need to get back to the children with an answer. Finally, adults need to listen to what children are saying and try to connect what they are saying to their recent experiences as well as to particular worries or fears. Children will talk in very informative ways if they feel that people are seriously listening to them.

6

"I Think the Law Is Right about Whales."

How to Help Children to Express and Extend Their Conceptual Knowledge about the World

Children's Critical Thinking

A primary goal of a developmentally appropriate preschool classroom is to encourage children to be active learners (Piaget, 1952; Vygotsky, 1962) and to become reflective (Dewey, 1933) and critical thinkers (Wertheimer, 1945). Children need to be helped to wonder, study facts, compare answers, evaluate their findings, and be ready to ask the questions that are at the next level. Unfortunately, many successful students are never taught to think critically (Brooks & Brooks, 1993).

When children are curious about the world around them, the good teacher acts as a facilitator and a guide. She does not always immediately answer children's questions. She takes a constructivist (Piaget, 1952; Vygotsky, 1962) approach to thinking about young children's learning. This approach stresses that children learn best when they are active in their learning and look for answers rather than passively hearing explanations from teachers. Teachers encourage children to be reflective and productive and to evaluate the evidence they gather as they develop ideas and concepts. Vygotsky's theory (1962) stresses the importance of the social context for learning. When the adult participates in the child's learning, she or he uses scaffolding to change the level of support she or he gives, according to the child's competence. This level of support can help children to move to a higher level of skill. When children have some undeveloped concepts, their curiosity is sparked. The adult can become a helper and can be someone who is more rational, logical, and organized. When adults take on a scaffolding role, the resulting dialog is important for developing the children's conceptual knowledge (Tappan, 1998). Vygotsky (1962) described the child's zone of proximal development as a range of ideas or problems that children cannot comprehend or solve alone, but can master with the help of adults. In order to help children move to a higher level of skill and knowledge, teachers must observe the present skill level of children and provide them with the necessary support. Thus, when the teacher provides children with appropriate scaffolding, their concepts develop and they reach a higher level of skill. Tharp and Gillmore (1988) found that children who participate in a classroom where teachers ask questions and encourage children to experiment with ideas and build their own concepts exhibit better attentional capacities and reading skills.

Wellman and Gelman (1992) posited that young children have three major theories about the world. They have a theory of mind (naïve psychology), a theory of the physical world (naïve physics), and a theory of living things (naïve biology). Wellman and Gelman proposed that these theories become elaborated during the early years of life. By age 3, children understand that there are internal mental states within themselves and others, that people have internal beliefs, and that peoples' wants and desires can be connected to their actions (Wellman & Gelman, 1992). Keil (1989) found that 3–4-year-old children have some basic biological concepts, including the understanding that plants and animals grow, can have offspring, and inherit properties or characteristics from their parents. Spelke (1988) demon-

Caitlin, Age 4, "Gerbil"

strated that infants know quite a bit about the physical world. They know about the permanence and movement of objects, and have an understanding of space as it relates to them. Thus, by the time children are 3 and are entering preschool, they have quite a bit of knowledge about their world. The classroom becomes a place where they can be helped to elaborate and refine this knowledge.

Classroom Meetings

Come into a classroom of 4- and 5-year-olds. They are gathered on the large rug of the classroom for their morning meeting. Some children sit on teachers' laps, others on small wooden stools, and still others are sitting cross-legged on the rug. They have already discussed the weather and marked the day on the calendar. It is the 32nd day of school, and they have posted the number 32 in its place just below the ceiling. By the end of the school year, the number cards go all around the room. Today, the children counted up to 32 by twos. Now, the teacher is asking the children whether they have anything to share. Several hands shoot up and the teacher calls on Nell.

NELL: I think the law is right about whales. Whales should not be killed because they are very important creatures of the sea.

TEACHER: Right, Nell. You are very concerned about animals.

NELL: Last night, we watched a movie about a circus that Daddy brought from the library. It gave me the idea to make a paper circus. First, we got paper, crayons, and poster paper and Daddy and I drew. I drew a lion and Charlie drew an elephant. We put them on the top of the tent. We didn't finish because it was too late to draw more animals.

TEACHER: You could make more animals here and take them home.

ZACK: Nell, I thought you were talking about whales, and then you talked about the circus.

TEACHER: She shared two pieces of information. Sometimes, when you are talking, you remember other thoughts you want to share. Why are whales so important? Why, Nell?

NELL: Well, it's like the time when the dinosaurs lived because whales are very big like dinosaurs were and this makes people think of those times that they don't want to forget.

TEACHER: Why else?

NELL: They are so gentle and playful.

TEACHER: How do we know that whales are gentle?

NELL: Because playful creatures are also gentle.

TEACHER: How do you know?

NELL: Whales and dolphins are gentle and playful, but sea cows are not playful but they are gentle.

TEACHER: How can you find out that whales are gentle and playful?

NELL: Maybe they are half sea cow and half dolphin child. Maybe a killer whale was attacking a penguin and a whale got in the way to stop it. It said that whales were gentle and playful on my dolphin tape.

TEACHER: You know from your tape, how else can we tell that whales are gentle?

ZACK: We also saw a show about whales.

RACHEL: There also used to be a whole lot of whales and now there are not.

TEACHER: How do you know when animals are not gentle?

RACHEL: Our neighbor's dog is not friendly and is always bothering us.

TEACHER: How do you know?

RACHEL: She barks and tries to jump on us.

TEACHER: Yes, you pay attention to signs that an animal gives, such as the dog that barks and jumps on you. People have paid close attention to the signs that whales give and have found out that whales are gentle.

RACHEL: Once, when we went to Florida by ourselves to visit our grandma, we saw a show with a killer whale who let a lady stand on his nose.

NELL: Once, I heard on my dolphin tape that there is another problem with killer whales. It's okay when they jump out of the water but it's not okay when they jump back in because they make a big splash.

TEACHER: Why is that a problem?

NELL: Well, it may splash in your face and the water they swim in is very salty and it may get in your eyes.

TEACHER: Do you think that children swim in water where whales are?

NELL: Maybe not so close to sharks but to dolphins or whales.

TEACHER: What kind of water did we learn that whales swim in?

SARAH: Salty water.

TEACHER: And what else?

ZACK: Deep water.

TEACHER: Right, deep water is usually where people don't swim.

RACHEL: Sharks and dolphins can't come on shore. If they did, they would die.

NELL: I know which sea creatures come near the shore. Clams. They come in with the waves. You can put your hands in the water and dig for them.

SARAH: I thought we were talking about how gentle whales are, not about sea creatures. Killer whales might not feel so good when they see a boat because they might think the boat will kill them. They might not know the boat has good people and then splash their tails against the boat because they want to sink it.

TEACHER: There are certain feelings that animals don't have and that's what makes people so special. Animals are different from people. We have to study, watch, observe, listen, and look for clues from them. They don't have the same feelings we do.

Meeting—A Time for Talking and Thinking.   While all of the children in the group did not make a comment during this lively discussion, they were all very attentive albeit some were a bit restless. They ended this meeting with a plan to study whales in more depth. The next day during meeting, the class listed some of the questions they wanted to address in their study of whales.

After observing this type of classroom meeting for a week, it becomes easy to see how such a regular activity in a classroom can give us a window into the cognitive, emotional, and experiential worlds of children. One can see in these discussions that the children are actively manipulating, transforming, and mastering information.

The Role of Meeting in the Curriculum.   The format and length of meetings in early childhood classrooms varies according to children's developmental levels and a teacher's plan for the curriculum. The teacher's role in the meeting also varies according to these same factors. A meeting can take a central role in a curriculum. It can help to build the community within the classroom. It gives children and teachers the opportunity to share ideas and thoughts. Children's comments about meetings are very revealing. "In meeting, people talk and talk and talk. Meetings are important. We learn lots of things." Meetings give children the opportunity to think and stretch their ideas about the world. They give teachers the opportunity to learn who children are, how they think, and what they think about. Consider the first example and the discussion about whales. Immediately, one sees differences in the ways Zack and Nell think about the world. Zack seems to like to focus on one concept at a time whereas Nell can become distracted by other thoughts. The teacher handled Zack's comment about Nell's style beautifully. Although she acknowledged how some ideas make you think about other ideas and validated Nell's style, she also validated Zack's style by returning to and expanding the discussion about whales. This kind of comment gives children permission to develop their individual voices and to see how their voice may differ from someone else's voice. In general, this gives children the idea that their thoughts and ideas will be accepted and discussed. They see firsthand that when they speak and share their ideas, they get feedback about facts—as well as about relationships.

Meeting Format.   Teachers usually plan for meeting to happen at the same time everyday. Usually, meeting takes place in the morning after children have arrived and have had a free play period. It can last from 5 to 30 minutes depending on the age of the children; their ability to focus, attend, and engage in conversation on that particular day; and the particular topics of conversation. It is best for meeting to begin with a predictable event. Most often, children and teachers work with a calendar and discuss the day, the month, the particular season, and the weather. Teachers often use this part of the meeting to informally teach some math concepts, such as counting the number of days children have been in school, graphing the weather for the month, counting the numbers of children present or absent, and counting the number of days left in the week. When the children count, they can do so by ones, fives, tens, or by any other number they choose. Teachers can choose to focus on topics such as more than, less than, and equal to, as well as addition and subtraction. Teachers can also use the discussion of weather to help children make observations about the weather and to ask questions about the causes of rain, thunderstorms, snowstorms, hurricanes, etc. Teachers can introduce children to the process of scientific inquiry and encourage children to ask questions, make observations, develop hypotheses, test these hypotheses, and draw conclusions.

Developing Ideas.   Children can be encouraged to engage in the process of scientific inquiry when they discuss the weather during meeting, but they can also be helped to discuss other topics they have explored. Consider the following excerpt from a meeting discussion about beehives.

TEACHER: What is a hive?

RACHEL: A hive can be paper or a different kind of hive with bark. Paper ones are called paper hives. Hives are very light and have holes in them. That's where the bees put their larvae.

TEACHER: You say they get bark for the hives. How do they get it?

TED: They hold onto it very good. They have to grind it up.

TEACHER: Yes, they have to grind it up. Good. How do they grind it up?

TED: They dig a hole in the tree and make sawdust.

TEACHER: How do they do that?

TED: They use their bodies.

TEACHER: Yes, they use their bodies, which part?

EVAN: Their mouth goes into a piece of wood and bites. They dig in and make a big hive.

ZACK: They have sharp jaws. They grind up bark with four very little sharp teeth.

TEACHER: Is bark all they use to build the hives?

TED: No.

TEACHER: What else do they use?

TED: Leaves, bark paper.

TEACHER: What else in nature do they use?

ZACK: Grass.

TEACHER: Yes, grass, lots of grass. They grind and spit out grass and the bees work to put layer on top of layer. Why do they make holes?

THREE CHILDREN IN UNISON: They put in larvae.

ZACK: No they don't, the workers don't put in the larvae. The queen comes and puts them in. The holes are not just for larvae. They are also for food. Bees don't just sting one thing and die. If the stinger gets stuck, they will die, but if it slides in and comes out, the poison case does not fall off.

PETER: Do people get poisoned from bees?

TEACHER: What do you think Zack?

ZACK: Just a tiny bit.

TEACHER: But not enough to get really hurt. Some people hurt and get a red mark.

The teacher sees Emily raising her hand. Earlier in the meeting she had wanted to say something, but when her turn came she declined to say anything.

TEACHER: Emily, did you remember what you wanted to share?

EMILY: Yes.

TEACHER: Go ahead and share your information.

EMILY: I've been having some bad days.

TEACHER: I'm proud of you for being able to say that, Emily.

EMILY: I'd like all of you to help me to not have so many bad days.

TEACHER: Yes, we really need to help one another. All of us need help to remember the rules every once in a while. Emily, you had a wonderful morning and a good day yesterday. We all need to help each other remember the rules.

The teacher really set the tone in this meeting that it is acceptable and safe to express one's ideas and feelings within the group setting. Clearly, during the discussion of bees, she, at different times, took on the role of listener, reflector, and extender of information, and at all times she led the children to express their ideas. Asking questions, such as what do you think, why, what did you see, and what do you think will happen next encourages children to consider the observations they have made in nature, books that have been read to them, and their own reactions to things. When Emily wanted to share her ideas that were not about bees, the teacher was very accepting and listened to her. This reaction would certainly encourage Emily to make more contributions to meeting. The teacher could have said, "Emily we are talking about bees right now," and Emily would have probably felt embarrassed and shamed. Instead, she felt as though she was a member of a community that cared about and helped one another and she felt safe enough to say that she was worried about having some bad days. (She had been aggressive and uncooperative.) Sometimes children need to express these worries before they are able to engage in discussion about other concepts. Thus, it is clear that when teachers plan a curriculum around meeting, they need to build it around the questions and theories they have heard the children express. They also need to listen to the conversations of children and always be aware of what is on their minds. A teacher may hear children arguing about something and she can say to them, "Let's have a discussion about that at meeting." Even during the rest of the day, teachers engage children in conversation about what they are doing. They may typically say things such as, "Tell me about your building." or "Tell me about your drawing." Once children respond, teachers can tailor the conversation so that the children share their ideas and thoughts. It is the children's ideas and thoughts that become the content for meetings.

Role of the Teacher.   Once the more structured part of the meeting is over, there is time for general conversation. Again, the topics for these conversations vary. Some programs have two to three different children per meeting share an idea or a thought, or ask a question. Sometimes, a teacher will introduce a topic of discussion. Sometimes, the meetings need to be stopped early because the children are not able to sit and listen. Sometimes, they need to be extended because the children are very involved in conversation. The teacher needs the flexibility to be able to gage how long a meeting needs to last. The teacher's role varies according to the developmental level of the children in the group. No matter what the age of the children, the teacher is always a model of speech for the children. His or her job is to ask open-ended questions and encourage the children to talk and to ask more questions. The teacher is always making sure that the children are wondering and conceptualizing and that the conversation is always organically connected to the children's interests and activities. The teacher is a listener, a reflector, and an extender of ideas. He or she keeps the children excited and curious about the topic of conversation. With younger children, it may be the teacher who asks the initial questions or introduces topics of conversation. Older children are usually raising and answering questions on their own.

Meeting Rules.   In the beginning of the year, the teacher sets down the rules for meeting. Sometimes, they even write down the rules and post them in the meeting area. Teachers will often introduce meeting as a time for the children to get together and share what they want to say. The major rules are that children need to sit down, raise their hands if they want to speak, and wait and listen when other children are talking. Children may have a difficult time sitting and a teacher may need to say to them, "Can you sit here, or do I have to choose a place for you?" If teachers can trust children's decisions, they eventually develop the capacity to sit and contribute to meeting.

Developmentally Appropriate Meetings.   Often times, if the class has a mix of younger and older children and is larger than 20, it is a good idea to split the meeting group in half so that the younger and older children can have separate groups. The meeting with younger children is more teacher focused. The teacher often introduces the topic of conversation. The goal for the younger children is for them to be trained in the art of meeting. What is important is that they get started sitting in a group and begin having discussions. A teacher may ask a simple question such as, "Do you like rainy days?" Consider some of the answers of the 3-year-old group.

> "Yes, because you get to stamp in puddles."
> "I like to catch raindrops on my tongue."

"I like to splash in puddles with my shoes and socks off."
"I like to play in the rain."
"No, because they always get me wet."
"I don't like getting my tights wet."

It is clear that the children in this group have clear opinions about rainy days and are able to express them. Because these are young children, they often do not stay on a topic so one child may have said something about snow instead of rain. It is not helpful for a teacher to say, "We are not talking about snow right now." Rather, a teacher might say, "You have some interesting ideas about snow, let's come back to that after we finish talking about rain." This comment about snow may spark a conversation about weather and the different conditions that exist for rain and snow. Through this comment, the teacher has gently told the child the importance of staying on a topic but has also acknowledged the child's idea as important so that he or she will continue to express his or her thoughts. Young children enjoy discussing topics that have some connection to them, such as, "Do you have a teddy bear?" or "Who is in your family?" or "What do you have in your room?" or "What is your favorite toy?" or "Do you have a pet?"

Older children, who have been trained in the art of meeting with the help of teachers, use their conversations to learn about a variety of concepts. Conversations may continue for weeks or only one meeting, depending on the particular interests of the children. The teacher gages the interest of the children and plans follow-up learning activities. Consider the following excerpt from a meeting:

TEACHER: Who has something to share? Pete?

PETE: My brother, Brian, gave me this crystal. It's real sharp up here.

RACHEL: That salt crystal fooled our daddy.

TEACHER: Why?

RACHEL: He thought it was a real crystal and it wasn't.

TEACHER: What makes a crystal a crystal?

NELL: Most are clear.

TEACHER: Are they different from rocks?

RACHEL: Yes, crystals are found in rocks.

NELL: Sometimes volcanoes make crystals.

WINNIE: How do they get inside rocks? Can you break any rock open and find crystal inside?

RACHEL: No, just some special rocks.

ZACK: Once, I broke a rock open. I found something red and it was a red crystal and once I smashed a rock and a crystal came out.

TEACHER: When we are outside we can explore some rocks and find out if all rocks have crystals. We can use hammers.

ZACK: Yeah, and goggles and that blue material to hold the rocks down.

It is clear from this conversation that the children have some knowledge about rocks and crystals. The teacher has asked them guiding questions to help them elaborate on their knowledge about rocks. She has also communicated that there is more to know about rocks and crystals. She is very knowledgeable about this topic, but instead of telling the children all her information, she has sparked their interest in finding out more about rocks and crystals by observing them and studying them. They will make their own discoveries and, along the way, the teacher will help them to describe their observations and discoveries.

Conclusion

In closing this chapter, it is important to remember that children do not have to be in a meeting at school to discuss and develop their conceptual knowledge of the world. They are always asking questions and are always curious. Discussions about these questions can also occur in small groups, at home with a parent, or alone at school with a teacher. Children's interests vary, and they may develop interests in areas in which adults do not feel they have any information. Adults can always say to children, "I don't know anything about that, but we can find out about it together." Children also do not need to have immediate answers to questions. Adults can say to them, "What do you think? Why?" In this way, children can become comfortable with making hypotheses. Some children may persist at saying that they don't know or may answer the question with the completely wrong answer. Then, adults may say to them, "That is an interesting answer. Let's look that up in a book in the library, and maybe we can find an answer." The goal for any of these conversations is for children to be encouraged to think reflectively and critically.

7 "I Am Going to Hate That Baby for the Rest of My Life."

Helping Young Children to Talk about Siblings and Birth

Four-year-old Jonathan's mother was expecting a baby. Although Jonathan had known about the pregnancy for a while, it was just becoming more obvious. His mother was a bit more tired than usual and lap sitting was becoming less comfortable for Jonathan. The "baby" always seemed to be in the way. Although Jonathan was a typical 4-year-old who struggled with aggression and was always quick to test the limits, recently it seemed as though all of his interactions with his mother, in particular, were aggressive and full of confrontation. One evening, when Jonathan and his mom were trying to go out, he refused to put on his shoes. His mother could not help him, and he was having a semitantrum rolling around on the floor and tossing his shoes out of his reach so he could not put them on. His mother had tried to be patient, understanding, and firm, but nothing was working except both Jonathan and his mom were becoming more and more frustrated. His mom said to him, "Jonathan, I am really tired of all of these fights. You have been fighting with me all day long and I am really angry and frustrated with you." Jonathan rolled around on the floor, kicked his legs, looked directly at his mother, and said, "I'm gonna hate that baby for the rest of my life." He gasped and blanched at saying that, but he looked immensely relieved when his mother replied, "It is hard to be having a new baby in our family. There are a lot of changes. You do not have to like the baby all of the time."

Kate, Age 4, "Bunny and Baby"

Jonathan quickly put on his shoes and said, "Let's go." His mother tried to talk with him more about his feelings about the baby, but he had said what he needed to and was not interested in hearing any more about the baby or asking about it. As the pregnancy progressed, he did continue to make comments about his ambivalence, and asked a number of questions.

Young Children and New Siblings

The birth of a sibling raises many questions, feelings, and concerns among preschool children. Children need to be helped to express these. Many times these questions, feelings, or concerns are expressed behaviorally as Jonathan did with his persistent fights. Adults often have to play the role of detective to determine what the children are expressing through their behavior. It is also the case that children's behavior does not always express their feelings about having a new baby. Although we can assume that some of their difficult behavior may be related to feeling ambivalent about a new baby, not all of it is. There are two major questions young children have when their mothers are expecting babies. The first one is what will having a new baby mean to the child and his place in the family? The second question, which often intimidates adults the most, is that children wonder where babies come from.

Children's Feelings about Becoming Older Siblings

Young children have a mixture of feelings and reactions to the idea of becoming older siblings. It is very normal for children to feel angry and jealous about this event. They also feel love and excitement. They see their parents' excitement and love, and they want to emulate that. They are also excited that they will be big enough to help to take care of the baby, and they feel the thrill of becoming more independent and self-sufficient. When a small helpless baby enters their lives, they can, maybe for the first time if they are first-born children, feel how big and competent they really are. All of these feelings can present them with conflict, both within themselves and between themselves and the outside world. It is the conflict or the ambivalence that they need the most help to express so that the adults in their lives can help them discuss it. Adults can do nothing to extinguish the conflict because it naturally occurs, but they can help children to see that it is a normal feeling and can help them to put some of their thoughts about the conflict into words so that they feel less overwhelmed.

Typical Conflicts about New Siblings

It is helpful to discuss the typical conflicts a young child feels as he or she is coping with the birth of a new sibling, but first it may be useful to describe some of the relevant literature. Just as children experience opposing feelings when receiving a new sibling, so the literature reflects these feelings when it examines sibling relationships. There is much literature that supports the positive influence that siblings have on development. Siblings have been found to contribute to the physical development of one another, and offer emotional support, nurturance, advice, and direction to one another (Stocker & Dunn, 1990). Younger siblings spend more time imitating their older siblings than their friends (Azmitia & Hesser, 1993). Despite the positive influences siblings have on one another, they also place demands and restrictions on one another (Stocker & Dunn, 1990). Findings have always indicated that sibling relationships are ambivalent, but there are usually factors that contribute to intensifying the negative side of the ambivalence. For example, if children have different or conflicting temperaments, their sibling relationship is often more difficult (Munn & Dunn, 1988). There is always conflict and increased hostility when there is parental favoritism or when parents treat children differently (Boer, 1990; Brody et al., 1992). Sibling relationships are seriously affected by the emotional climate of the family. Children are more likely to fight when parents are not getting along (Hetherington, 1988). First-born children often exhibit extremes in their reactions to the birth of a sibling. Some become more demanding, others become more independent and take a role in the care of the sibling, and some become detached from their mothers (Dunn, 1984). Thus, children have a variety of reactions to the birth of a new sibling. Their reactions are affected by the emotional climate of the family, their particular temperament, and their parents' reactions to the sibling. Despite these different reactions, all children with new siblings deal with very similar conflicts and it is to these that we now turn.

Ambivalence. There are several conflicts that children experience when they are coping with the birth of a new sibling. These conflicts are constantly being revisited as both siblings grow and develop. One conflict is that of feeling a mixture of love and hate for the sibling.

When the child's loving feelings dominate, there is often no reason to believe that the child is feeling anything other than unconditional love for his sibling. But it is easy to see the ambivalence when a gentle hug becomes a squeeze that has the baby gasping for breath. After all, this baby is an intruder in the child's life. Some children are overly loving toward their siblings. Although this is nice for adults to see, it is often the case that children who are this nice to their siblings are fighting hard not to acknowledge the negative side of their ambivalence. This does not extinguish the anger, and the child does not learn to cope with his ambivalence in the sibling relationship. In fact, the negative feeling may be acted out in some other way. One 3-year-old girl, Amy, was very excited about being a big sister. She talked about how she was a big girl now and how she was going to help her mother and father take care of the baby. She was very attentive, loving, and gentle with the baby. Her parents thought she was just the model sister and were so relieved they did not have to struggle with her anger. They encouraged her "good" behavior. After a few weeks of this model behavior, Amy began to be a bit clingy and whiney. Her parents were tired after being up at night with the new baby and left out some cold medicine. Amy ingested some of the medicine and had to go to the hospital to have her stomach pumped. Amy's parents were terrified and were helped to realize that they did not have to expect her to be a perfect older sister and that she could feel jealous, angry, and upset about the baby. As she was given permission to express some of her negativity, she was less attentive to her sister and was even able to sometimes say, "I wish that baby wasn't borned," and when her parents heard this they were able to say to her, "It is hard to have a new baby come into the family." When children fight against the negative side of their ambivalence, they often do so because they do not like feeling out of control and they fear they will lose the love of their parents if they express their anger more freely. They are often relieved when parents or other adults express, in general, how young children feel about having new siblings. Some of the following statements are very helpful to hear and give permission to children to feel what they are feeling.

> "Sometimes children get very angry when the baby seems to be getting all of the attention."
> "It is hard when the baby never seems to stop crying."
> "I know you don't like it when Mommy can't go outside with you right when you want her to."

Once children hear statements like this, they are able to put some of their confused feelings into words. Jonathan, who was going to hate that baby for the rest of his life, said to his mother a few weeks after his baby brother was born, "I really hate it when you nurse the baby." Then his mother engaged him in a conversation about how long she would nurse the baby, how she nursed him when he was a baby, and what he used to be like. For a while, Jonathan wanted to have a bottle while his mother nursed the baby, but he soon lost interest and was too busy and interested in other things to sit long enough to finish a bottle.

Conflicts about Growing up. A second conflict children have when they are experiencing the birth of a new sibling is the conflict between wanting to grow up and wanting to remain a baby. Although regression is a normal and healthy part of development, parents fear the regression of their older child when the newborn is putting such stress on their caretaking abilities. Parents who rush to get their older toddlers out of diapers and cribs and into underwear and big beds are often concerned and worried when they want to return to their cribs and start having toileting accidents soon after the baby is born. Even without having to deal with the birth of a new sibling, young children constantly struggle with the idea of whether they want to hold onto their newfound independence and become more self-sufficient or whether it is easier to be a baby. The problem for them is that they wish and fear for their independence almost as strongly as they wish and fear for their dependence. They love their independence and are so proud of their new skills, but being independent can be both lonely and scary when it involves interacting in a world that is full of mostly bigger and stronger people, and objects and ideas that are often not fully understood. They work so hard at being independent and self-sufficient that they often need to regress and refuel before they can venture out again. They can also be very jealous of the attention the new baby receives and may think that the life of a dependent baby is what they long for. What they learn is that they do not want to be so dependent that they lose their newfound independence, and end up feeling angry and frustrated because they cannot have both, and their parents cannot do anything to make them feel less conflicted. It is this anger and frustration that leads to a regression in behavior, an increase in testing the limits, and an increase in tantrums. It is this conflict that adults need to help children talk about so that they can express their confusion and frustration.

Emily, Age 4, "My Dad"

It is not helpful to say to a preschooler with a new sibling, "Oh, only babies wear diapers," when he has a toileting accident or asks for a diaper. It is also not helpful to say, "Oh, you are not a baby anymore; you don't need a bottle. Mommy needs you to be her big boy." But what is helpful to say to children when they, as they typically do, ask to have a bottle or a diaper? Some parents will say no and others will allow children to have them. This can be an individual parent's decision. There is no absolute right or wrong decision to make regarding this request. What is most important when children ask to have baby things is that the adults engage them in conversation about the feelings and conflicts they are experiencing that are causing them to want these things. Some of the following comments are helpful.

"You know big kids, even grown-ups, have baby feelings sometimes."

"Sometimes it is hard work being the big sister all of the time, and maybe you don't always feel like helping with the baby."

"Sometimes your baby feelings make you feel like having a bottle, and sometimes having a bottle does not make your baby feelings go away."

"Sometimes it is hard work learning so many new things, and it is o.k. to take a break from the hard work and just have a story with mom or dad."

"I spend time with the baby when I am giving her a bottle, but you and I can spend time together in another way. Maybe you could think of a way we could spend time together when the baby is asleep."

"What do you like about having a bottle?"

"I wonder why you are wanting a diaper?"

"Maybe sometimes you wish you were still a baby."

All of these statements assure children that what they are feeling is normal and acceptable. They also encourage children to express their thoughts and ideas and to explore their reasons for wanting things.

Where Do Babies Come from?

The second main question young children struggle with when they are faced with the birth of a new sibling is, "Where did the baby come from?" They want to know how the baby got in their mother's belly and how it will get out. We are not being honest with our children if we prolong the myth that babies are brought by the stork and appear miraculously. Often, the older siblings are preschoolers when a new baby is born, and the pregnancy becomes a topic that arouses children's curiosity about sexuality, gender differences, and gender roles.

How to Talk about Birth. Adults feel uncomfortable talking about sex and birth with young children and are often reluctant to do so. Children do not feel this level of discomfort; in fact, they are very curious about everything in their world. Children between the ages of 3 and 5 are in a phase of development where they have a keen interest in sexual differences. They are interested in their own genitals. They are curious about what they do and how they feel. They are curious about the differences between boys and girls. They engage in normal exploration and masturbation. They experience excitement and curiosity about sexual ideas and concepts. They get very silly if they see another child in the bathroom, and they get very excited when they talk about "private parts." They also are very interested in relationships between men and women, and they can become especially silly if they see adults expressing physical affection toward one another.

Preschool children also worry about their own power and competence, and they particularly feel small and ineffectual in relation to just about everyone else in their world. They will often act out around these worries. They can be typically controlling, bossy, and frustrated because they cannot do the grown-up things they wish they could do. They appropriately try on adult roles in their play, and they can get some feelings of competence and potency through this play. The reality for them though is that it is the adults who can have the babies and not them. Thus, when confronted with the question of how babies are made and born, they experience a mixture of curiosity, anxiety, jealousy, and envy. At these times, the reactions of important adults to both their questions and behavior are crucial.

When young children ask adults about babies or sexuality, adults often feel anxious and unsure about what to say. Just when one thinks he or she is prepared for all questions, a child asks one that leaves the adult thinking that he or she does not know how to answer it. It is always helpful to respond to a child's question with a question. Asking, "What do you think?" will give children the ability to express their ideas about a particular topic. Then the adult can either elaborate on accurate information, or correct distortions. For example, when children ask how the baby gets out, they often think the baby will be born when the mother goes to the bathroom. With this information, the adult can say, "When babies are born they come through the birth canal and out through the vagina. That is a different place from where pee and poop come out." Some children are satisfied with that. One usually knows they are satisfied if they say something such as, "Oh, that's how," and then do not ask any more questions. It is usually a good idea to determine whether they have further questions before giving them more information. If they do not have any more questions, it is often useful to say, "You might have some more questions later so just let me know." It is important not to overwhelm them with information, and it is always best to gage from their reactions how much more information they need at the moment. It is also important to remember that when a child asks an adult a question that the adult is not sure how to answer, the adult can say, "I need to think about that for a little while before I give you an answer. I will get back to you on that." Then, it is important that the adult follow up with an answer.

How Did the Baby Get There?   Probably the question that adults feel most uncomfortable about answering is, "How did the baby get there?" or "How do you make a baby?" Again, in order to respond to this question, adults first need to know what children think. Preschoolers respond to this question with a number of theories. Some of these include the following.

> "My mommy ate a lot of food and she made a baby."
> "My mommy and daddy told God they wanted a baby so they gave them one."
> "I told mommy and daddy I wanted a baby sister so they ordered one."
> "Mommy and Daddy hugged and made a baby."
> "Daddy gave Mommy a seed to swallow and she made a baby in her belly."

Some of these statements have some accurate information, but they are far from completely accurate. Once adults know what children's theories are, they can answer their questions more effectively. In answering the question about how babies are made, it is important not to overwhelm children with information. It is important to answer simply and accurately. Here is one example of how an adult could answer a young child who asks how babies are made.

"A baby is made by a man and a woman. A man's body carries sperm in his penis and a woman's body carries eggs in her ovaries. When they want to make a baby, the man puts his penis inside the woman's vagina and releases sperm. When a sperm and an egg join together, they start to grow into a baby. It takes a long time for the egg and the sperm to join together and then grow into a baby. The baby grows inside the mother in a special place called the uterus or the womb. After a long time, 9 months, which is almost as long as from your birthday this year to your birthday next year, the baby is ready to be born. The mom's body knows when it is time for the baby to be born, and the muscles in the uterus start to push the baby out through the birth canal. The doctor helps the mom push the baby out in the hospital and is there to make sure that both the mom and the baby are healthy. This is a lot of information, and you still might not understand it. We can look at some pictures or some books if you like, and you might still need to ask some questions."

Preparation for the Birth. It is often helpful for a preschool child whose mother is pregnant to accompany her to the doctor one or two times during the pregnancy. It is helpful for children to hear the baby's heartbeat, to feel it move and, to maybe see some ultrasound pictures. Simple pictures of a developing fetus can also be a useful aid. Whenever children are exposed to new information, it is often helpful to ask, "What did you think about hearing the baby's heartbeat?" or "What do you think of those pictures? Do you have any questions about them?" Children may not have comments at the moment, but it is important to listen for their ideas as they talk with their friends or play with their toys. It is important to find the balance between overwhelming them with information and avoiding or ignoring their questions. They need to know that we are accepting of their questions no matter what they are about.

Conclusion

Thus, there are two main questions young children have when they are about to become older siblings. They are concerned about what will happen to their place in the family and whether they will still be given enough attention and care. They feel vulnerable and may be very dependent and clingy until they adjust to the change in the family structure. Young children are also curious about how babies are made and how they are born. They have many of their own theories about these events, and they need help correcting their theories and answering their questions. They are better equipped to address their affective reaction to becoming an older sibling when they are clear about the factual information and when the information is presented to them in a way that helps them to feel that they have some cognitive control over a situation that feels very much out of their control.

8

"This Is Very Important. When I Am Four and I Am a Man, I Will Get a Car."

How to Talk about Issues of Self-Esteem While Helping Preschoolers to Express Their Wishes and Disappointments

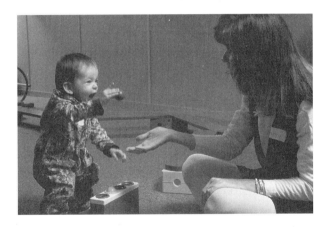

Supporting the Development of Self-Esteem

Spend a week watching children, and try to identify the observations that make you smile and think, "Everything is all right with that child." They will probably be observations in which the child is smiling and exuding a sense of mastery. Think of the child who has just learned to walk. All he wants to do is walk. His arms are outstretched, he is leaning over his feet a bit, and his feet move forward trying to keep up with his enthusiasm over his newfound power. Although he does not have the words to express what he is experiencing, he seems to be saying, "Look what I can do! Here I come world!" His enthusiasm is contagious and one cannot help but smile and take delight in this newly developed skill. Listen to toddlers who exclaim, "Me do!" or "Do again!" Watch toddlers insist on doing things for themselves. Watch them smile and jump up and down and even flap their hands when they complete a challenging task. Listen to preschoolers who say, "I can do it by myself." or "Watch and see how high I can pump on the swing." or "I think I can do the hard one." One can conclude from watching these children that they feel very good about themselves, and that they are on their way to building a powerful sense of self-esteem. Often, parents' major wish for their children is that they do develop a positive sense of themselves. A statement often echoed by parents is, "I just really want her to feel good about herself." How is it that some children develop a positive sense of themselves and others do not? How do you talk to young children so you have a sense of what they are feeling about themselves? How do you help young children to be realistic in their expectations for themselves as they experience their wishes and disappointments?

Self-Esteem and Young Children

Parents are absolutely right in knowing that a child's self-esteem is a very important factor in healthy development. Studies (Harter, 1988, 1999) of self-esteem have found that high self-esteem in childhood is connected to satisfaction and happiness in adulthood. Conversely, low self-esteem in childhood is connected to depression, anxiety, and maladjustment in school and later relationships. The challenge for adults who interact with young children is to know how to support the development of a positive sense of self-esteem. In order to know how to do this most effectively, it is important to understand some developmental principles and to understand the results of research that have described the parental characteristics that lead to high self-esteem in middle childhood.

The Drive toward Progressive Development.   All children are motivated to move forward in their development. Some do so at different

Cassie, Age 4, "Beautiful Fairy Princess"

rates, but it is easy to observe this drive whether one watches a 12-month-old learning to walk or children in kindergarten trying on the roles of adults in their play. Theorists differ when they describe the source of this motivation. Robert White (1960) aptly described it as "effectance, the motivation to explore, manipulate, and master the world." After repeated experiences with such exploration, manipulation, and mastery, children develop feelings of competence. It is these feelings of mastery or competence that build a positive sense of self-esteem. When the drive toward progressive development is not present in a child, it is easy to see his lack of investment in developing competence and one questions what has gone wrong in the child's development to cause this arrest.

Supporting Children's Struggles with Dependence and Independence. Young children's growing autonomy and independence can only develop and thrive if they have developed trusting relationships with significant caregivers. It is through these relationships that they develop a sense of trust in themselves and others and are given the ability to become more separate and independent. Even though they are interested in being independent, they still need to know that they can come back to that secure base and refuel and regress if necessary. Sometimes, this ambivalent behavior is confusing for adults who interact with children. Children engaged in the struggle over dependence and independence need to know that this is a normal struggle. They need to feel accepted by the adults. The kind of comment that does not communicate this acceptance is something such as, "Oh, you went off and left mommy, and now you want to come back and be friendly." or "Oh, you don't have to act like a baby." A child is more likely to feel accepted and able to talk about the conflict over dependence and independence if the adult makes comments such as, "Sometimes it is hard to know if you want to be a big boy or a baby. Sometimes it is just too hard to be a big boy all of the time." It is this kind of acceptance by the parent or other adults that has been found to be a characteristic that supports the development of self-esteem in children (Coopersmith, 1967).

There are many times when the acceptance of the child is easy. For instance, when they are happy, involved, and compliant, this task is very easy. It is when they are irritable, clingy, stubborn, and provocative that it becomes more difficult to be accepting. It is important to note that being accepting does not necessarily mean that the adult allows the child to engage in the latter behavior to an extreme. Rather, the accepting adult is able to acknowledge and accept the affect behind the difficult behavior and, at the same time, communicate that she or he does not condone difficult behavior such as kicking, hitting, screaming, etc. The unaccepting adult shames the child for his or her behavior. For example, "Stop clinging. You are a big girl and you do not need to do that, and you are going to make me fall." The accepting adult is able to communicate expectations without shaming the child. For example, "I know you are feeling nervous about coming to a new place. But I am going to stay with you, and I can help you better if you can hold my hand and talk with me about what is worrying you." Although the child may not be able to say anything at the moment, he or she has at least been understood and given some strategies to use to cope with a difficult situation. The child has also learned that it is possible to talk about difficult situations.

The Importance of Clear Limit Setting. Another factor found to support the development of self-esteem in children is the ability of adults to set clear limits for children (Coopersmith, 1967). Setting limits for children becomes a challenge during the second year. It is during this year that children have a growing sense of autonomy and independence. They usually wish for omnipotence both in themselves and the adults in their lives. They often try to obtain this omnipotence by wanting to be the boss of everyone and everything. You can hear the words as early as 15 months, which emphatically state "Mine." "Me do." "No." Some older and somewhat more articulate 2-year-olds might express the wish for omnipotence quite clearly. "Because I want everyone to do what I want them to do." At 18 months, children recognize their reflections in the mirror, and between 18–24 months they begin to refer to themselves with pride. As they recognize themselves as independent, they begin to make plans on their own and begin to see that sometimes their plans and activities are not what the adults want them to do. As they test the limits, they develop a growing sense of what is right and what is wrong as appropriate limits are set for them. Even though they test the limits constantly, they long to be accepted and loved in the eyes of the important adults in their lives. The limits need to be set in such a way so that the children gradually realize they cannot be omnipotent, nor for that matter can the adults. Whenever limits are set, children are helped if they are not shamed for testing the limits, and if adults can help the children to find an alternative activity that might help them feel competent. For example, children who keep trying to play with the pots on the stove may be able to satisfy the urge to be like mommy or daddy when they cook by having their own drawer of pots and cooking utensils that they can play with while their parents are cooking. Children who are given the cooking utensils to play with have at least experienced that their urge to be like mom and dad is a good one and one that is valued by the people that they love. This kind of confirmation of one's wishes clearly leads to the building of self-esteem.

Parents' Respect for Individuality. A third factor (Coopersmith, 1967), which has been shown to be linked to the development of self-esteem in children, is the parents' respect for children's individuality. Children who feel that they can be themselves and have their own interests, even if they are different from their parents, are usually able to develop a positive sense of self.

Preschool Children's Wishes to Be Grown-Ups. When children exit toddlerhood and enter the world of preschoolers, they usually have reached some resolution about their wishes to be omnipotent. Those who have done so successfully feel positive about their growing independence as well as their growing competencies. They begin to feel very grown up. They wish to be like grown-ups. Remember the 3-year-old boy who announced proudly to his mother, "When I am four and I am a man, I will get a car." They focus quite a bit of their play on trying on the roles of adults. Thus, you see preschool classrooms in which family scenarios are played out. Usually the biggest struggle children have in this play is deciding who will play the roles of mother and father. Most of the children are vying for this role and work very hard to resolve the conflicts connected with this dilemma. The other kind of play that is most often seen in preschool classrooms is that in which children are taking on the roles of superheroes. They are constantly battling large and dangerous foes and ending the battles in victory. They do not have much time to enjoy the victory because battles begin anew. This play may seem very limiting and repetitive, but it often has an important purpose. Because preschool children wish to be like the grown-ups in their world, they are constantly disappointed by the fact that they are smaller, less powerful, and less competent than the adults. The more they experience these disappointments, the more tenacious they may become in their interactions with adults and in their insistence in playing these games of superheroes in which they are the grown-ups in control. Their wish to be bigger and stronger is often so powerful that adults interacting with these children feel they have to limit the power the children seem to have. They may even feel compelled to struggle with the children over who really is bigger, stronger, and in control. The delicate dance that adults have to perform is to be able to set limits for children when appropriate while helping them face their disappointments without jeopardizing their self-esteem.

Just as limit setting and respect of children's individual styles is important to the building of self-esteem in toddlers, it is just as important in interactions with preschool children. Three-, four-, and five-year-olds have better developed language skills than toddlers. They can use their language to express their feelings and describe their experience of themselves. They can use the models adults give them to make some sense of their confused and conflicted feelings when they experience disappointments and conflict. Adults often mistakenly think that young children should not experience conflict or disappointment, and they offer children only praise and constantly try to bend over backwards so that children will develop a positive sense of themselves. Actually, this kind of approach to supporting a child's self-esteem usually leads to children who are unhappy and unable to tolerate conflict or disappointment. They do not feel comfortable being in charge of everything and push harder for limits, structure, and a more realistic assessment of their strengths and weaknesses. Self-esteem does not develop in children who are duped into thinking that they and their world are perfect, because no one is perfect. Children who do not experience conflict or disappointment are not able to develop strategies to cope with failures or disappointments and may often be devastated when they have such an experience. The result of this can lead to children feeling depressed and not positive about themselves at all.

Children's Reactions to Limit Setting and Adult Expectations. It is clear that children watch adults very carefully. Children are exquisitely aware of adults' reactions to them. It is the adults in children's lives who provide them with the standards against which children measure themselves. If adults expect children to be perfect, then children will feel that they can never measure up to these impossible expectations. If adults cannot set limits for children, children will not develop their own set of inner controls and will not feel good about themselves as they continue to test limits, looking for someone to support them in developing self-control. There are many ways in which adults can talk with children about their wishes and disappointments, as well as their developing sense of themselves. When they do this, it is important to talk with children in such a way that they know that the adults are interested in their ideas, reactions, and feelings.

Helping Children to Talk about Conflicts

Because children at different ages are struggling with different conflicts, it is important to be able to address them around their developmental struggles. If they successfully negotiate their developmental struggles, then they gradually build their self-esteem. The more success they have at each developmental level, the more able they are to take on the challenges of the next level. Nobody completely resolves conflicts and developmental tasks, but children develop personality traits and coping strategies, which help them to address these developmental challenges. They are helped to address these challenges when they are encouraged to talk freely about their thoughts and feelings. Although there is no specific script adults can follow as they are talking with children about their developing sense of themselves within the context of their developmental challenges, there are some ways to think about addressing some of the issues and challenges from one developmental level to the next.

The most important thing to remember when talking with children about their wishes and disappointments and their developing self-esteem is to listen to them first and not immediately tell them they are not able to do something because they are too little or not strong enough. Clearly, children need to be protected from doing things that are too dangerous and beyond their capabilities, but if they are told no as soon as they express their idea, they may feel that they cannot have such ideas and wishes and may feel they cannot do anything well. Adults need to set limits for children, but they can do so within a context that acknowledges the child's thoughts, feelings, and ideas and offers children a perspective on what they are capable of doing and how they are growing, changing, and learning. Let's turn to some specific examples from children in both the toddler and the preschool phases of development.

Toddler Conflict.   Toddlers are often heard saying, "No!" "Me do." and "Mine." They get into struggles with their parents when they cannot have their own way, and they can have very long, drawn-out tantrums when they do not get their way. They wish and long for omnipotence, and they become disappointed when neither they nor their parents have such power (Mahler, 1975). They are very persistent in trying to get such power, but they are always relieved when someone sets a limit for them. They go through a process in which they gradually give up the wish for omnipotence as they develop a sense of independence and more reasoning in their thinking, and when they are helped to feel confident and competent about their developing skills. Sometimes, when toddlers are at their most tyrannical, adults feel that they have to get into a struggle with them and often want to follow the impulse to say, "I'm the boss. You cannot be the boss. You are too little." Although it is true that the adult is the one who must ultimately be in charge, these kinds of statements shame young children and tend to make them feel that they cannot have their own wishes and ideas.

What Adults Can Say to Struggling Toddlers.   There are things adults can say to toddlers that will allow them to feel all right about the wishes they have, but that will, at the same time, help them to develop a more realistic sense of themselves and their world. Adults can say to a toddler who insists on being the boss of everything and everyone something such as, "You wish you could be the boss of everyone." The child may respond with something such as, "I am the boss." The adult could respond with, "Yes, you are really learning to be a good boss of yourself. You can be the boss of your toys and some of the things you like to do. You cannot always be the boss, and I have to help you or stop you from doing something that I think is not safe." Adults can also say, "Sometimes, the grown-ups have to help children when they are having a hard time being good bosses for themselves." These kinds of statements acknowledge children's wishes and desires and also give them an opportunity to respond with questions or a restatement of their wishes. While children may be disappointed because they cannot run the world, they will not be made to feel ashamed about having those wishes and will begin to see how they can achieve a part of their wish by developing their own competencies and hearing from others how they are growing and learning. It is important to know that children need to hear these comments from adults many times and in many different situations. The development of self-esteem and the ability to develop appropriate expectations of oneself is an ongoing process.

Helping Preschool Children to Talk about Conflict. As children move out of toddlerhood and into the preschool years, they begin to experience a whole new set of developmental challenges. Children of this age are curious about everything. As they are further refining their sense of themselves, they begin to be very aware of the differences among their age-mates. They become interested in the differences between boys and girls and men and women. They are also exquisitely interested in the world of adults. They want to be like adults, and they may often look like little adults in their play as they imitate the important adults in their lives. The difficulty they have is that their attention is being constantly brought to the fact that they are not adults and that, in fact, they are very small and impotent compared to the adults they know. This does not stop them from trying to find ways of being more like their parents or older children they know. Consider the 4-year-old boy who wants to wrestle with his dad. He will often go into the wrestling match believing that he can actually win the match, but very soon he becomes aware of his father's strength and power and how little he is in comparison. If his father is truly holding back in the match, the boy may become hopeful that this time he will be victorious and intensify his efforts to the point that he either hurts his father or challenges his dad enough so his dad then feels he has to win the wrestling match. More often, the end result is the little boy feeling that he is little and not very powerful. Although this is a disappointment for a child, it does not necessarily mean that his self-esteem will suffer. Children will have reactions to such disappointments that they need to talk about and express their longings about, and there are ways in which adults can help them to do this.

What Adults Can Say to Preschool Children Who Wish to Be Grown-Ups. When preschool children insist that they can do what grown-ups do, adults can respond in such a way so that they do not extinguish the hope the children have about getting bigger. Sometimes, children can be so aggressive and provocative in their bids to be grown-ups that adults are pushed to make very unhelpful comments such as, "No, I am bigger than you and you cannot do that." or "You are not a grown-up. You are only a little girl and little girls do not get married." Just as adults need to help toddlers to develop a more realistic perspective on the subject of their omnipotence, so they also need to help preschoolers realize that they can be competent, strong, and mature without actually being adults. It is always useful to talk with children about how much they wish for something. For example, it is helpful to say, "I know you really wish you could be a grown-up, and you are upset because you cannot always do what the grown-ups do." It is also helpful to give children some hope by saying, "Someday, you will be a grown-up and you will be very big." The child may respond, "But I am a grown-up." The best way to respond to such a comment is with something such as, "Yes, you do wish so much to be a grown-up that sometimes it seems that you already are." It is also helpful for adults to give children a perspective on how rapidly they are growing and changing. Adults can say things such as, "Not so long ago, you did not know how to climb on the climber and you needed mommy to push you on the swing. Now you can do those things all by yourself. That is really a sign that you are getting to be a bigger girl." They can also comment on their children's physical growth. "At one time, you weren't able to reach the sink without standing on the stool, and now you can. You are really growing." Adults can also encourage children to think about the world of grown-ups. They can say, "I wonder what

James, Age 5, "Me"

you will like to do when you become a grown-up. I wonder what your children will be like." Comments such as this encourage children to value their own ideas and wishes. They also give children the opportunity to think and respond, which gives them some feeling of control; and children have the opportunity to think about their unique qualities and interests. Helping children to value their own ideas and wishes also builds on children's developing sense of themselves as individuals. When children respond to these questions, adults can have a deeper look into their inner worlds.

Conclusion

The development of self-esteem is a very important component of healthy development. Children are naturally motivated to move forward in their development. They need trusting relationships, appropriate limits and expectations, and the experience of being appreciated and accepted for their individual thoughts, feelings, and ideas in order to develop a positive sense of themselves. Adults need to constantly help children to develop appropriate expectations for themselves by engaging them in conversation about their ideas and wishes. Adults always need to acknowledge wishes and help children see that although they are not adults they are still able to be competent, strong, and mature in a way that is developmentally appropriate.

Concluding Remarks

Talking about Difficult Issues

This book has focused on discussing how children talk about difficult issues. It examines the important developmental issues one needs to consider to respond to children when talking about difficult issues and the role adults can play to help children to feel comfortable enough to express their thoughts and ask questions about difficult issues.

In order for children to develop the ability to talk comfortably about issues such as birth and death and fears and anger, there are certain developmental supports and accomplishments that make this task proceed smoothly. Children feel comfortable expressing themselves if they have experienced a consistent and predictable caregiving environment in which they have formed solid attachments to loved ones. Ideally, they have had support in expressing feelings and developing inner controls, and they have been allowed to be curious and active in their learning. They feel they can express their ideas and ask their questions and adults will not be put off, embarrassed, or uncomfortable with their comments. Children can and will talk about difficult issues if adults listen, respond, and communicate interest in ways that help children to talk more and, perhaps, cope with a difficult situation.

Talking about Fears

Children have fears, some of which are typical for their developmental level and some which are idiosyncratic. If their fears are acknowledged and not dismissed or denied, they will feel they can tell us more.

Talking about Anger

Children experience intense anger. They need help to know it is normal to be angry and that being angry does not mean that they are bad. They need help to develop inner controls and to express their feelings in words and not in actions. This development of the ability to both express and control expressions of strong feelings happens gradually. Children can successfully achieve these inner controls if they are given firm and consistent limits, if adults understand and acknowledge their feelings, and if adults do not use physical punishment or humiliation.

Talking about Death

Young children view death as a natural event in their world and are curious about it. Death becomes a relevant topic for them as they struggle with their own feelings of separation and loss as they work on becoming more independent. Many adults think that talking about death with children will be too overwhelming for them. It is much better to talk about death with children as they raise questions about it than to avoid the topic. Young children read adults' underlying affects very well. If adults communicate that death is a topic that is off limits, then children will not ask the questions they need to ask in order to feel less anxious. If children experience a loss, they need to be helped to understand that the loss brings with it (for themselves and others) a mix of complex feelings including sadness, anger, and anxiety. Young children do not yet have a universal, final, and irreversible concept of death. If they do experience a loss as a young child, then they typically need to rework and revisit the loss as they proceed through other developmental stages.

Talking about the World

Children are curious and need to be active learners. They need support to think critically and reflectively about their world. Adults can provide children with the scaffolding or support they need to develop their conceptual knowledge of the world. They are capable of engaging in serious discussions in which they explore concepts of psychology, physics, and biology through asking questions, generating hypotheses, and exploring data. These discussions and explorations can take place in group meetings at school as well as in individual conversations between children and parents and teachers and children.

Talking about Birth and Siblings

The birth of a new sibling is an event that arouses a young child's curiosity and anxiety. Children are anxious about what is unknown about an impending birth. First, children are concerned about losing their position in the family, and they deal with a mix of feelings over becoming an older sibling. They need to be able to talk about and express both the positive and negative feelings they experience when anticipating the birth of a sibling. Young children are very interested in bodies and are naturally very curious about how babies are made and born. They need to be able to ask their questions and must be given the information they need to begin to answer their questions.

Talking about Self-Esteem

Young children are working on developing a sense of themselves as separate and independent. They feel proud as they master new skills every day, and yet they long to be bigger, stronger, and more grown-up. Although they are not yet grown-ups, they can be helped to feel competent about what they can do. They can be helped to both express disappointment and maintain wishes and dreams about being grown-ups.

How Adults Can Be Good Listeners

The first step adults need to take in being able to listen effectively to young children is to take the time to watch children at play and in interaction. It is important to watch behavior and just as important to attempt to observe children's affective response to situations. One will see individual styles among children. A major question adults need to constantly ask themselves is, "How can I understand what this child is experiencing right now?" Sometimes this is very clear but other times there are inconsistencies between a child's behavior and his or her feelings or experience of the event. When listening to a child, it is important to have the confidence that you are hearing what the child needs to say or ask. When children feel heard, they will continue to ask questions and share information and feelings that reflect on their experience.

Children do ask questions that make adults feel uncomfortable and unsure. Instead of trying to ignore the questions, adults can say, "You have some difficult questions. I am not sure how to answer them right now. Let me think about it for a while and then we can talk some more about it." They can also say, "What are your thoughts about that question?" After an adult has had a conversation with a child about a difficult topic, he or she may say, "You may have more questions about that later. Just let me know, or I might ask you about it in a few days."

Finally, there are three important points to remember when listening to and responding to the questions of young children. First, always be honest. Do not give children misinformation because you think they cannot handle the thought of death or of an overwhelming fear. Children depend on us to be honest with them and it becomes a basis of their trust in themselves and others. Second, the answers and explanations we give must match the developmental level of the children engaged in conversation with us. Third, it is important to know that we do not need to overload children with information. We need to watch and listen to determine when they have the information they need at the moment. There will always be other opportunities for them to ask both old and new questions. If they have felt listened to and responded to, children will continue to feel that they can discuss their ideas, thoughts, and feelings with responsive adults.

REFERENCES

Ainsworth, M. D. S.; Blehar, M. C.; Walters, E.; & Wall, S. (1978). *Patterns of attachment.* Hillsdale, NJ: Erlbaum.

Azmitia, M.; & Hesser, J. (1993). Why siblings are important agents of cognitive development: A comparison of siblings and peers. *Child Development, 64*, 430–444.

Bates, E. (1976). *Language and context. The acquisition of pragmatics.* New York: Academic.

Biber, B. (1963). *Play as a growth process.* New York: Bank Street Publications.

Bornstein, M. H. (1999). *Culture, parents, and children: Intranational and international study.* Paper presented at the meeting of the Society for Research in Child Development, Albuquerque.

Bowlby, J. (1969). *Attachment and loss* (Vol. 1). London: Hogarth.

Brazelton, T. B. (1983). *Infants and mothers: Differences in development.* New York: Delta.

Bretherton, I.; & Beeghly, M. (1982). Talking about internal states. The acquisition of an implicit theory of mind. *Developmental Psychology, 18*, 906–921.

Bridges, K. (1932). Emotional development in early infancy. *Child Development, 3*, 324–341.

Brody, G. H.; Stoneman, Z.; & Burke, M. (1987). Child temperaments, maternal differential behavior, and sibling relationships. *Developmental Psychology, 23*, 354–362.

Brooks, J. G.; & Brooks, M. G. (1993). *The case for constructivist classrooms.* Alexandria, VA: Association for Supervision and Curriculum Development.

Brown, M. W. (1938). *The dead bird.* New York: Dell.

Burns, S. M.; & Brainerd, C. J. (1979). Effects of constructive and dramatic play on perspective taking in very young children. *Developmental Psychology, 15*, 512–521.

Campos, J. J.; Caplovitz, K. B.; Lamb, M. E.; Goldsmith, H. H.; & Sternberg, C. (1988). Socioemotional development. In M. M. Haith & J. J. Campos (Eds.), *Handbook of child psychology: Vol. 2, Infancy and developmental psychobiology* (4th ed., pp. 783–915). New York: Wiley.

Chess, S.; & Thomas, A. (1977). Temperamental individuality from childhood to adolescence. *Journal of Child Psychiatry, 16*, 218–226.

Chomsky, N. A. (1976). *Reflections on language.* London: Temple Smith.

Connolly, J. A.; & Doyle, A. B. (1984). Relations of social fantasy play to social competence in preschoolers. *Developmental Psychology, 20*, 797–806.

Coopersmith, S. (1967). *The antecedents of self-esteem.* San Francisco: W. H. Freeman.

Curry, N. (1985). Where have all the players gone? In Curry, N. (Ed.), *The feeling child: Affective development reconsidered.* New York: Harworth.

Dansky, J. L. (1980). Make believe: A mediator of the relationship between play and associative fluency. *Child Development, 51*, 576–579.

Dewey, J. (1933). *How we think.* Lexington, MA: D.C. Heath.

Dunn, J. (1983). Sibling relationships in early childhood. *Child Development, 54*, 787–881.

Dunn, J.; Bretherton, I.; & Munn, P. (1987). Conversations about feeling states between mothers and their young children. *Developmental Psychology, 23*(1), 132–139.

Dunn, J.; & Kendrick, C. (1982). *Siblings.* Cambridge MA: Harvard University Press.

DYG, Inc. (2000). What grown-ups understand about children: A national benchmark survey (sponsored by Civitas, Zero to Three, Brio).

Eisenberg, N.; & Fabes, R. A. (1998). Prosocial development. In N. Eisenberg (Ed.), *Handbook of child psychology* (5th edition). New York: Wiley.

Erikson, E. H. (1950). *Childhood and society.* New York: Norton.

Ervin-Tripp, S. (1991). Play in language development. In B. Scales, M. Almy, A. Niculopoulou, & S. Ervin-Tripp, *Play and the social context of development in early care and education* (pp. 184–198). New York: Teachers College Press.

Essa, E. L.; & Murray, C. I. (1994). Young children's understanding and experience with death. *Young Children, 49*(4), 74–81.

Fabes, R. A.; Eisenberg, N.; Jones, S.; Smith, M.; Gutherie, I.; Poulin, R.; Shepard, S.; & Freidman, J. (1999). Regulation, emotionality and preschoolers' socially competent peer interactions. *Child Development, 70,* 432–442.

Feinman, S.; & Lewis, M. (1983). Social referencing at 10 months: A second-order effect on infants' responses to strangers. *Child Development, 54,* 878–887.

Freud, A. (1936). *The ego and mechanisms of defense.* New York: International Universities Press.

Freud, A. (1946). *The psychoanalytical treatment of children.* London: Imago.

Freud, A. (1965). *Normality and pathology in childhood: assessments of development.* New York: International Universities Press.

Furman, E. (1990). Mothers, toddlers and care. In S. Greenspan & G. Pollock (Eds.), *The course of life* (vol. 2, pp. 61–82). Madison, CT: International Universities Press.

Goldsmith, H. H.; & Gottesman, I. I. (1981). Origins of variation in behavioral style: A longitudinal study of temperament in young twins. *Child Development, 52,* 91–103.

Gottman, J. M.; Katz, L. F.; & Hooven, C. (1997). *Meta-emotion: How families communicate.* Mahwah, NJ: Erlbaum.

Greenacre, P. (1960). Considerations regarding the parent–infant relationship. *International Journal of Psychoanalysis, 41,* 571–584.

Harlow, H. F. (1959). Love in infant monkeys. *Scientific American, 200,* 68–86.

Harter, S. (1983). Cognitive-developmental considerations in the conduct of play therapy. In C. Schaefer & K. O'Connor (Eds.), *Handbook of play therapy* (pp. 95–127). New York: Wiley.

Harter, S. (1986). Processes underlying the construction, maintenance, and enhancement of the self-concept in children. In J. Suls & A. Greenwald (Eds.), *Psychological perspective on the self* (vol. 3). Hillsdale, NJ: Earlbaum.

Harter, S. (1998). The development of self representations. In W. Damon (Series Ed.) & N. Eisenberg (Vol. Ed.), *Handbook of child psychology: Vol. 3, Social, emotional, and personality development* (5th ed.), pp. 553–617. New York: Wiley.

Harter, S. (1999). *The construction of the self.* New York: Guilford.

Harter, S.; & Whitesell, N. (1989). Developmental changes in children's understanding of simple, multiple, and blended emotion concepts. In C. Saarni & P. Harris (Eds.), *Children's understanding of emotion* (pp. 81–116). Cambridge: Cambridge University Press.

Hetherington, E. M. (1988). Parents, children and siblings: Six years after divorce. In R. A. Hinde & J. Stevenson (Eds.), *Relationships within families* (pp. 311–331). Oxford: Oxford University Press.

Izard, C. E. (1991). *The psychology of emotions.* New York: Plenum.

Izard, C. E.; & Malatesta, C. Z. (1987). Perspectives on emotional development: Differential emotions theory of early emotional development. In J. Osofsky (Ed.), *Handbook of infant development* (2nd ed., pp. 494–554). New York: Wiley.

Katz, L. F. (1999). *Toward a family based hyper vigilance model of childhood aggression.* Albuquerque, NM: The Society for Research in Child Development.

Keil, F. C. (1989). *Concepts, kinds, and cognitive development.* Cambridge, MA: MIT Press.

Mahler, M. S. (1975). *The psychological birth of the human infant.* New York: Basic.

Michalson, I.; & Lewis, M. (1985). What do children know about emotions and when do they know it? In M. Lewis & C. Saarni (Eds.), *The socialization of emotions* (pp. 117–139). New York: Plenum.

Parens, Henri. (1989). Towards a reformulation of the psychoanalytic theory of aggression. In S. I. Greenspan & G. H. Pollock (Eds.), *The course of life* (pp. 129–161). Madison, CT: International Universities Press.

Parten, M. (1932). Social play among preschool children. *Journal of Abnormal Social Psychology, 27,* 243–269.

Pepler, D. J.; & Ross, H. S. (1981). The effect of play on convergent and divergent problem solving. *Child Development, 52,* 1202–1210.

Piaget, J. (1952). *The origins of intelligence.* New York: International Universities Press.

Piaget, J. (1962). *Play, dreams and imitation.* New York: Norton.

Provence, S.; Naylor, A.; & Patterson, J. (1977). *The challenge of day care.* New Haven and London: Yale University Press.

Robertson, J. (1953). Some responses of young children to the loss of maternal care. *Nursing Times, 49,* 382–386.

Rogers, C.; & Sawyers, J. (1990). *Play in the lives of children.* Washington, DC: National Association for the Education of Young Children.

Rothbart, M. K.; & Bates, J. E. (1998). Temperament. In W. Damon (Ed.), *Handbook of child psychology* (5th ed., vol. 3). New York: Wiley.

Schonfeld, D. J.; & Smilansky, S. (1989). A cross-cultural comparison of Israeli and American children's death concepts. *Death Studies, 13,* 593–604.

Shonkoff, J. P.; & Phillips, D. (Eds.). (2000). *From neurons to neighborhoods. The science of early childhood development.* Washington, DC: National Academy Press.

Singer, J. (1972). *The child's world of make believe.* New York: Academic Press.

Speece, M. W.; & Brent, S. B. (1984). Children's understanding of death. In C. A. Corr & D. M. Corr (Eds.), *Handbook of childhood death and bereavement* (pp. 29–50). New York: Springer.

Spelke, E. S. (1988). The origins of physical knowledge. In L. Weiskrantz (Ed.), *Thought without language.* New York: Oxford University Press.

Sroufe, L. A. (1979). Socioemotional development. In J. Osofsky (Ed.), *Handbook of infant development.* New York: Wiley.

Stenberg, C.; Campos, J.; & Emde, R. N. (1983). The facial expression of anger in seven-month-old infants. *Child Development, 54,* 178–184.

Stocker, C., & Dunn, J. (1990). Sibling relationships in adolescence. In R. M. Lerner, A. C. Peterson, and J. Brooks-Gunn (Eds.), *The encyclopedia of adolescence.* New York: Garland.

Strassberg, Z.; Dodge, K.; Pettit, G.; & Bates, J. (1994). Spanking in the home and children's subsequent aggression toward kindergarten peers. *Developmental Psychopathology, 6,* 445–462.

Tappen, M. B. (1998). Sociocultural psychology: Exploring Vygotsky's "hidden curriculum." *Educational Psychologist, 33,* 23–33.

Tharp, G. R.; & Gillmore, R. (1988). *Rousing minds to life: Teaching, learning, and schooling in social context.* New York: Cambridge University Press.

Walden, T. (1991). Infant social referencing. In J. Garber & K. Dodge (Eds.), *The development of emotional regulation and deregulation.* New York: Cambridge University Press.

Wellman, M.; & Gelman, S. A. (1992). Cognitive development: Foundational theories of core domains. *Annual Review of Psychology, 43,* 337–375.

Wertheimer, M. (1945). *Productive thinking.* New York: Harper.

White, R. (1960). Competence and psychosexual stages of development. *Nebraska Symposium on Motivation* (pp. 97–106). Lincoln: University of Nebraska Press.

Vygotsky, L. S. (1962). *Thought and language.* Cambridge, MA: MIT Press.